The Early American Cookbook

Authentic Favorites for the Modern Kitchen

Dr. Kristie Lynn and Robert W. Pelton

© Kristie Lynn and Robert W. Pelton, 1983
LIBERTY PUBLISHING COMPANY
Cockeysville, Maryland

Second Printing: February, 1987

Published by:

Liberty Publishing Company, Inc.
50 Scott Adam Road
Cockeysville, Maryland 21030

Library of Congress #83-81148
ISBN 0-89709-047-0

Manufactured USA

Dedicated to

some of the earlier members of our family—the Peltons, Mitchells, Collisters, Northrups, Daniels, and Tylers;

and especially to

Barnabus Horton of Leichestershire, England, who came to America on the ship *Swallow* some time between 1633 and 1638 with his wife Mary and two children, Joseph and Benjamin. They landed at Hampton, Massachusetts, and were Puritans;

and also to

Great-great-grandmother Huldah (Radike) Horton, one of the finest and most famous horsewomen of her day. She rode with Lafayette in a parade in his honor in Newburgh, New York, in 1824. The French General and friend of the young country was making his second and last visit.

To be a good cook means the knowledge of all fruits, herbs, balms and spices, and of all that is healing and sweet in field and groves, and savory in meats; means carefulness, inventiveness, watchfulness, willingness and readiness of appliance. It means the economy of your great-grandmothers and the science of modern chemists. It means much tasting and no wasting.

Ruskin

Contents

Page

Preface 1
Introduction to Cooking in America. 3
Authentic Colonial Cookery. 11
Favorites of American Patriots 23
The Jefferson Family 37
The First First Lady—Martha Washington. 47
Traditional Early New England 57
A Taste of the Old West. 71
Indian Style Food Preparation 83
Traditional Old Southern Flavor 95
Authentic Recipes of Plantation Mammys 107
The Original Midwestern Taste 117
Presidential Parade of Favorites. 129
America's Earliest Cooking School 141
The Boston Cooking School of 1879 149
Bibliography of Interesting Old Cookbooks 159
Old-Time Measurements 163
Index 165

Preface

The recipes presented in this book have been selected with regard to their applicability to modern cooking methods as well as for their historical value. Some are traditional family specialties from the long-forgotten past. Others were gleaned from cook books used throughout early America. A number had been laboriously inscribed by hand on yellowed, stiff and cracking ledger pages. Still others were written in old notebooks dating back before the American Revolution and the signing of the Declaration of Independence. The final recipes bring us up to just beyond the American Centennial in 1876.

Here you may try favorites of presidents and vice-presidents and First Ladies. You may serve dishes enjoyed by the military leaders of both the Revolution and the War Between the States. You may cook specialties of black mammies on old plantations and of chuck-wagon chefs at round-up time in the Old West. Prepare the same hearty foods once eaten in forts of the colorful western frontier, and on staid New England farms. Eat traditional foods made by mountain folk in many locales, and by yesteryear's housewives in bustling mid-western homes.

The first recipe in each chapter is presented exactly as it first appeared in an old cook book or manuscript, and then repeated in its modern adaptation. All subsequent recipes in the chapters appear only in their adapted format. Some chapters conclude with poetic recipes in their original form.

You can use the recipes with complete confidence. They represent some of the finest cooking and warmest hospitality in America, from colonial times up to the end of the nineteenth century. They are still the basis of good, wholesome, family cooking today.

AMERICAN COOKERY,

OR THE ART OF DRESSING

VIANDS, FISH, POULTRY and VEGETABLES,

AND THE BEST MODES OF MAKING

PASTES, PUFFS, PIES, TARTS, PUDDINGS,
CUSTARDS AND PRESERVES,

AND ALL KINDS OF

CAKES,

FROM THE IMPERIAL PLUMB TO PLAIN CAKE.

ADAPTED TO THIS COUNTRY,

AND ALL GRADES OF LIFE.

By Amelia Simmons,

AN AMERICAN ORPHAN.

PUBLISHED ACCORDING TO ACT OF CONGRESS.

HARTFORD:

PRINTED BY HUDSON & GOODWIN.

FOR THE AUTHOR.

1796.

The first cook book ever written by an American and published
in the United States.

Cooking In America

The progress of the culinary art in America is an achievement of generations. We owe our modern methods of cookery to the sturdy and inventive pioneer mothers, predominantly of English, German, and Dutch origin, whose constant devotion to preparing food well has been continued by their daughters, until our present level of home cookery was finally reached. There was no higher evidence of good housekeeping in colonial days than the production of a perfect, tasty meal.

Happily, the reputation of our foremothers in cooking still lingers as a powerful influence in the housewifery of today. To say that the art of cookery is passing from the home to a commercialized industry is to malign the skill of today's homemakers. More and more, they are turning to the wholesome arts of their great-grandmothers and their mothers before them, taking pride in setting before their families the home-prepared dishes so-called convenience foods can never equal.

Modern food supply distribution makes today's cook's task easier. The colonial cook often found it necessary to substitute what was at hand for the ingredients she lacked. But an abundance of natural foods—wild fruits and berries, game, wildfowl, fish, maple syrup and wild honey, offset this lack. All of these were common foods for rich and poor alike. In the pre-Jamestown diary of Captain Arthur Barlowe, he noted that there were "large forests overrun with deer, rabbits, hares, and woodfowl in great abundance."

In the seventeenth century publication *Leah and Rachel*, colonial Virginia was characterized as follows:

> Cattle and Hogs are every where, which yeeld beef, veal, milk, butter, cheese and other made dishes, porke, bacon, . . . these with the help of Orchards and Gardens, Oysters, Fish, Fowle and Venison, certainly cannot but be sufficient for a good diet . . . considering how plentifully they are.

The settlers had found the Indians cultivating corn as well as sweet potatoes, squash, peanuts, beans and wild rice. They also captured and bred wild turkeys and tapped maple trees for sap to boil down into delicious syrup. The newcomers added these and other New World delights to the foodstuffs they brought with them from their homelands.

The first formal cook books used in America were reprints of those published in England. The earliest known to have been reprinted in this country was called *The Compleat Housewife; or, Accomplish'd Gentlewoman's Companion*, by E. Smith. It was published by William Parks, Williamsburg, in 1742, and soon became extremely popular.

Even after this volume was reprinted again, in 1764, cook books continued to be a rarity in America. At this time, most recipes were still handwritten and handed down through families or exchanged between friends. Passing from lady to lady as a personal gesture, they might bear such touches of exquisite care in the making as "wash the butter free of salt, and flavor it in a bath of rose water," and the secret of secrets—"a dash of vinegar to the rose water gives piquancy to the flavor." And so it does.

Homemakers of those early days were expected to know exactly what to do with the ingredients called for in any recipe. Most hand-me-down recipes merely listed the ingredients. No instructions accompanied the lists. Early cook books were often written in the same fashion, with such inexplicit directions as "add water" or "put in a little white wine." How much water? How much wine?

The housewife was expected to already know these things without being told. An excellent example of this can be seen in a recipe from *The Compleat Housewife* for "Apple Pastries to Fry":

> Pare and quarter Apples, and boil them in Sugar and Water, and a Stick of Cinnamon, and when tender, put in a little White Wine, the Juice of a Lemon, a Piece of fresh Butter, and a little Ambergrease or Orange-flower Water; stir all together, and when 'tis cold, put it in Puff-paste, and fry them.

Polenta was the name the Indians gave to corn meal. Simple corn meal mush was known in early colonial times as "Indian Pudding" and sometimes "Hasty Pudding," for good reason. The following recipes for "A Nice Indian Pudding" are taken from *American Cookery* by Amelia Simmons, believed to be the first cook book ever written by an American. It was published in this country in 1796.

> No. 1. 3 pints scalded milk, 7 spoons fine Indian meal, stir well together while hot, let stand till cooled; add 7 eggs, half pound raisins, 4 ounces butter, spice and sugar, bake one and half hour.
>
> No. 2. 3 pints scalded milk to one pint meal salted; cool, add two eggs, 4 ounces butter, sugar or molasses and spice q.s. it will require two and half hours baking.
>
> No. 3. Salt a pint meal, wet with one quart milk, sweeten and put into a strong cloth, brass or bell metal vessel or earthern pot, secure from wet and boil 12 hours.

Big ovens of brick, always ready for the baking, had been left behind in their old homes by the settlers. In the new land bricks were scarce. There was little known clay obtainable for brick-making. Certainly none along the desolate shores of the broad Atlantic where the Pilgrims landed. And the colonists were not at first equipped to manufacture bricks. So the Pilgrim mothers did their baking either in Dutch ovens of tin, set facing the open fire on the stone hearth with a tin shield to ward off the flames, or in an iron kettle with squat legs and a depression in the cover for hot coals to give the top heat.

Fresh meats, at this early period, were often roasted on a spit before the open fire, while salted meats (or "corned" as this process of curing was called) were boiled in kettles with pot hooks hung from the swinging crane inside the deep cooking hearth. Vegetables, combined with these boiling meats, made the soups and stews of which the Yankee was so fond. At first, hams were cured, and bacon smoked, and various meats pickled in the home. It wasn't long before such items could instead be acquired from nearby farms.

Later, fireplaces with brick wall ovens were used for baking. Wood continued to be the primary fuel used. Baked foods were put in "slow" to "quick" or "hot" ovens "until done," "until tender," or "until enough." The method of measuring oven heat in the seventeenth and eighteenth centuries was simple but effective. If the heat was excessive, it scorched the inquiring hand.

Cooking on the open hearth was still the most common method through the early 1800s.

Vegetables were almost always served cooked. Tomatoes, or, as they were called, "love apples," were thought to be poisonous. Caster sets (containers for vinegar, oils, pepper and other condiments) on the table provided a variety of seasonings to suit each diner's taste. Corn (maize) was known as a native grain during the colonial period. The Indians called it *pagstowr*; the English settlers referred to it as "Guinea Wheat" or "Turkey Wheat." It was first used by the colonists for making breads and for stuffing fowl.

Farmyards produced eggs in abundance, and flour was a local production. All that was needed to transform the raw materials into a delicious meal was the experience and skill of the housewife, and it was seldom lacking. With the simplest of equipment, she fed her family well and appetizingly.

Sugar was purchased in large, round-topped loaves (called "loaf sugar") up until the late 1800s. A chunk, as needed, was then sifted and passed through a sieve before it was ready for use in cooking or baking.

Up until the 1800s, butter was always salted, and the salt had to be washed off before use in much of the cooking. Later it bacame available either salted or unsalted. Here's how Amelia Simmons told the homemaker of 1796 to buy and store her butter, long before refrigeration as we know it.

> To have sweet butter in dog days, and thro' the vegetable seasons, send stone pots to honest, neat, and trusty dairy people, and procure it pack'd down in May, and let them be brought in in the night, or cool rainy morning, covered with a clean cloth wet in cold water, and partake of no heat from the house, and set the pots in the coldest part of your cellar, or in the ice house. Some say that May butter thus preserved, will go into the winter use, better than fall made butter.

Early desserts did not differ greatly from the sweets enjoyed today. Tarts—pastry shells filled with preserved fruits or jellies—were a favorite. Puddings, including custards and steamed puddings for special occasions, were served with sweet sauces. Dessert jellies were popular and the earliest congealing agent used in the colonies was gelatin made by boiling down calves' feet.

Isinglass (a gelatin extracted from the air-bladders of certain fish, not mica) later came into popularity during the 1800s, but most good cooks long preferred to use the old familiar "calf's foot jelly." It was considered to have better taste and consistency. Explicit directions for making good gelatin from calves' feet can be found in almost every pre-1900 cook book.

Another very early British cook book, Markham's *Countrey Contentments* was widely used in America around 1700. It offers these requirements for a good cook and homemaker:

> First, she must be cleanly, both in body and garments; she must have a quick eye, a curious nose, a perfect taste, and a ready ear. She must not be butter-fingered, sweet-toothed, nor faint-hearted; for the first will let everything fall, the second will consume what it should increase, and the last will lose time with too much niceness.

The most popular of all early cook books in 1760-1770 Virginia was also of British origin. This book had an unbelievable title: *The Housekeeper's Pocket-book, and Compleat Family Cook: Containing Above Twelve Hundred Curious and Uncommon Receipts in Cookery, Pastry, Preserving, Pickling, Candying, Collaring, &c. with Plain and easy Instructions for Preparing and Dressing every thing suitable for an Elegant Entertainment, from Two Dishes to five or Ten, &c. and Directions for ranging them in their proper order.*

Another popular English cook book was first reprinted in 1772, in Boston, after Paul Revere made the plates for it. This one was titled *The Frugal Housewife or Female Companion*, by Susannah Carter. It was dedicated to "those who are not ashamed of economy."

In 1805, *The Art of Cookery Made Plain and Easy*, by A Lady (later identified as Hannah Glasse) was printed in the city of Alexandria, Virginia. It, too, had been published originally in England, in 1747. British editions of this book were extremely popular in America during the eighteenth century. The author offered:

> Amongst the various arts which most essentially contribute to the gratification of the human species, there is none more deservedly worthy of attention than cookery; or the art of rendering a dish of victuals as palatable as possible will certainly be deemed of considerable importance to all.

Mistress Mary Randolph was reputed to be the best cook in Richmond in the late 1700s. Her book's slogan was simply "Method is the Soul of Management." In the preface of *The Virginia Housewife*, published in 1824, she wrote:

> Management is an art that may be acquired by every woman of good sense and tolerable memory. If, perchance, she has been bred in a family where domestic business is the work of chance, she will have many difficulties to encounter; but a determined resolution to obtain this valuable knowledge will enable her to surmount all obstacles. She must begin her day with an early breakfast, requiring each person to be in readiness to take their seats when the muffins, buckwheat cakes, etc., are placed on the table.

Doughnuts were originally known as "olykoeks" (oily cakes) in the colonies. They were later called "Yankee Cakes" in the south of the early 1800s. An interesting recipe from *The Virginia Housewife*, titled "Dough Nuts—A Yankee Cake" is as follows:

> Dry half a pound of good brown sugar, pound it and mix it with two pounds of flour, and sift it; add two spoonsful of yeast, and as much new milk as will make it like bread: when well risen, knead in half a pound of butter, make it in cakes the size of a half dollar, and fry them a light brown in boiling lard.

Between 1820 and 1860, the black iron stove came into vogue, as did ice boxes and cast iron sinks. They remained, however, luxuries to most families. One extremely interesting cook book of this era, published in 1842 at Cleveland, Ohio, was titled, believe it or not, *Everybody's Cook and Recipe Book: But More Particularly Designed For Buckeyes, Hoosiers, Wolverines, Corncrackers, Suckers, and All Epicures Who Wish to Live With the Present Times.*

The kitchen at Sunnyside, home of Washington Irving, has a mid-18th century wood-burning stove. Just to the left of the stove is a copper boiler fed by soft flexible lead pipes and its water is heated by the stove. The table is of the late 17th century and of Hudson River valley origin. *Courtesy of Sleepy Hollow Restorations, Tarrytown, New York.*

Most canning in 1800 America was still done at home, by covering the jars with brandy-soaked paper and then by other newer methods of capping them. Stone or earthenware crocks were commonly used for preserving fruits. Before the mid-1800s, home preserving was the only way a family could enjoy most fruits and vegetables when they were out of season. Some winter vegetables would keep in a root cellar, of course. Can openers came into their own when the stores for the first time, in the middle of the nineteenth century, began to stock the newly-developed commercial canned goods (using metal cans and sealing tins). By 1860, over five million cans of food (mostly tomatoes, but little meat) were being marketed annually.

Oleomargarine was often sold as butter to the unsuspecting housewife of the late 1800s. It was at that time simply butter adulterated with beef fat, and according to one highly-popular old cook book, *Bread, Cake and Cracker Baker:*

> The cheaper kinds of butter are frequently adulterated with common wheat flour, starch, oatmeal, pea-flour, lard, and are sometimes mixed with suet and turnips, as well as with a large quantity of salt and water.

Theories about natural foods, and distrust of chemical additives, are nothing really new; they were of grave concern to some cook book writers of the nineteenth century. Mrs. Horace Mann, for example, wrote one she called *Christianity in the Kitchen, A Physiological Cook Book.* In this remarkable work, the author condemned the use of baking soda and saleratus by saying, "Our stomachs were not made to digest metals, and when we ponder them and eat them we try to cheat nature."

Juliet Corson set a landmark for culinary artistry when she opened the country's first cooking school in 1874 (the basis of Chapter 13). Corson taught a very popular course called "Demonstrative Lessons in Cookery." Mary Lincoln soon followed suit, starting the "Boston Cooking School" in 1879 (recipes from this source form Chapter 14). Her enterprise later became famous under the guidance of Fanny Farmer.

The late 1800s saw the introduction of gas cookery. The ice box and the cast iron sink became more commonplace. Commercial ice houses sprouted up all over the bustling nation. By this time the "Dover" egg beater was replacing the now old-fashioned "whisk." Kitchens, and the good things that came out of them, were beginning to approach in look and in methods of preparation, the kitchens of today.

Authentic Colonial Cookery

The legend of the American colonists is one we crave and savor as if it were an epicurean delicacy. The romance of the thought-to-be-simplistic early days lives on and on, in spite of frequent reminders of the way things really were—dangerous, grueling, lonely, more boring than adventurous. But we will not let go of the heroic visions, suns setting over miles of untouched wilderness, and wild animals or Indians—or both—behind every rock and in every crevice.

And who does not have fond memories of legendary dishes of days gone by—food cooked within an open fireplace using a variety of iron, copper and brass pots, pans and utensils. The estimable cook's volume of dainty delectables is unsurpassed even today. However, "cooking from scratch" in our generation is an almost forgotten art. Who can resist trying such old-time delights as Oglethorpe's Molasses Cake? Endicott's Cheese Pudding Dinner? Winslow's Ham and Egg Pie? Or even Loudoun's quaint Apple Pudding? All of these treats were in their day considered to be the last word in cookery.

Sir John Wentworth's Colonial Onion Soope
Cut a plate full of thin slices of Bread, and sett them before ye fire to Crisp. Then cutt about half a Dozen of Middle Size Onions into bits, boyle half a pound of Butter Stiring it well till it be very red and have done frothing and then put ye Onions to it, and boyle them till they begin to turn Blackish, Still stiring of them, to this put about 2 quarts of water, and thicken it with 2 yolks of Eggs, then break ye Bread into small pieces and put it in with Some Spice & a little Salt, when it is ready pour in some Lemon Juce, or a Spoonfull or two of Vinegar if ye like it.

Sir John Wentworth's Colonial Onion Soup

2 tablespoons butter
6 medium onions, chopped fine
6 cups water, boiling
2 egg yolks, beaten
1 tablespoon salt
1 teaspoon pepper
6 slices bread, toasted
2 teaspoons lemon juice
          or
2 teaspoons vinegar

Melt the butter in a large cast iron skillet and when hot, fry the chopped onion until it begins to turn yellow. Stir this into the pot of boiling water and allow to simmer for 20 minutes. Stir the beaten egg yolks into the pot of hot liquid and let it thicken. Now add the salt and pepper. Break the toast into small pieces and stir this into the soup. Let it simmer for another 3 minutes. Lastly, take the pot from the stove and stir in the lemon juice or vinegar. Cover and let stand for 2 minutes. Serve while very hot and still steaming.

Sir John Wentworth graduated from Harvard College in 1755 and was the Colonial governor of New Hampshire from 1767 to 1775.

Rebecca Motte's Mashed Parsnips

6 large parsnips
4 tablespoons cream
2 tablespoons butter
1 teaspoon salt
1/2 teaspoon pepper

Put the whole parsnips into a cast iron kettle of cold water. Bring to a boil and cook until tender. Then drain well, and scrape off the skin. Mash the parsnips with the back of a large wooden spoon. Pick out all of the stringy fibers and throw away. Now blend in the cream, butter, salt and pepper. Put this mixture into a saucepan and bring to a boil. Take off the stove and beat hard. Heap into a mound on a platter and serve while hot.

Rebecca Motte is a little known Colonial heroine. She came over from England and married Jacob Motte, a South Carolina planter in 1758. She was a widow at the beginning of the Revolutionary War. The British drove her out of her mansion and named it Fort Motte. Rebecca agreed to burn the mansion down in order to dislodge her unwelcome guests. She bought an Indian bow and arrows, hired an expert to fire the lighted arrows, and accomplished her task.

REBECCA MOTTE.

Joseph Reed's Early American Coffee Ice Cream

1/4 pound ground coffee
2 cups cream
2 cups milk
1 cup sugar

Put the coffee, cream and milk into a double boiler. Bring to a boil and immediately remove from the stove. Let it stand until cold. Strain and then blend in the sugar. Put into a container and freeze.

Joseph Reed was an active patriot who lived in Philadelphia in 1770. He was instrumental in the detection of treason in the dealings of General Arnold and was the man who forced bringing the General to trial. He died in 1785, having served for a number of years as president of Pennsylvania.

Colonial Potato Omelet—A William Penn Favorite

1/2 cup milk
1 teaspoon flour, heaping
1 cup potatoes, mashed
1 teaspoon salt
1/8 teaspoon pepper
3 egg yolks, well beaten
3 egg whites, stiffly beaten

Smoothly blend the milk and flour in a saucepan. Stir in the mashed potatoes, salt and pepper. Gently stir until the mixture is free from lumps. Pour this over the beaten egg yolks and beat rapidly. Lastly, whip the frothy egg whites into this mixture. Heat and butter a cast iron skillet, and quickly pour the omelet into it. Fry until the underside is browned. Set the skillet on the rack in the oven (400 degrees) for a few minutes to brown the top. Serve immediately.

William Penn will always be remembered as the founder of Pennsylvania. He was a Quaker who was born in London in 1644. He was given 45,000 square miles of land in payment of an $80,000 debt the crown owed his father. He had to pay an annual rent of two beaver skins to Charles II, for what was known as Penn Sylvania.

WILLIAM PENN.

Molasses Cake Specialty of James Oglethorpe

JAMES EDWARD OGLETHORPE.

1/2 cup sugar
1/2 cup shortening
1 egg, well beaten
1 teaspoon cinnamon
1 teaspoon ginger

1/2 cup molasses
1/2 cup sour milk

1/2 teaspoon baking soda
3 cups flour
2 teaspoons baking powder

Cream the sugar and the shortening in a large wooden mixing bowl. Add the beaten egg, cinnamon, ginger, molasses and sour milk. Dissolve the baking soda in 1 tablespoon of hot water. Add this to the mixture in the bowl. Blend all of these ingredients well. Sift the flour and the baking powder together, twice, and add to the bowl. Turn into a well-greased and floured cake tin. Bake in a moderate oven (350 degrees) for 30 minutes.

James Edward Oglethorpe is remembered as the "father" of Georgia. He was born in London, 1698, and was granted a charter in 1732 by King George II for the purpose of founding the colony of Georgia. Oglethorpe accompanied the first group of emigrants and in 1733 founded the city of Savannah.

George Fox's Quaker Pudding Dessert

2 eggs, separated
6 tablespoons sugar
1/4 cup flour
1/4 teaspoon salt
3/4 teaspoon baking powder

2 cups milk
1 1/2 teaspoons ginger
1 1/2 teaspoons powdered sugar
1/2 teaspoon vanilla

Beat the yolks of the eggs with the sugar for 10 minutes. Then sift the flour with the salt and 1/2 teaspoon of the baking powder. Stir this into the egg-sugar mixture. Scald the milk and pour it slowly into the bowl, stirring all the time. Dump all of this into a large saucepan and stir over a low heat until it forms a thick custard. Lastly stir in the ginger and pour into a buttered baking tin. Beat the egg whites with the remainder of the baking powder until they are frothy. Add gradually, while still beating, the powdered sugar and vanilla. Spread this meringue on top of the custard and place in a very moderate oven (325 degrees) for 20 minutes, or until lightly browned. Serve cold. This recipe makes enough for 6 people.

George Fox was the founder of the Society of Friends, or Quakers. He was born in 1624 and came to America in 1672, to preach in Maryland, Long Island and New Jersey.

Edward Winslow's Ham and Egg Pie

EDWARD WINSLOW.

4 eggs
1/4 teaspoon pepper
1/4 teaspoon baking powder

1/2 cup milk
2 cups ham, cooked and cubed
1 cup cheese, grated

Beat the eggs in a wooden mixing bowl and quickly stir in the pepper, baking powder, milk, ham and cheese. Pour this mixture into an unbaked pie shell. Place in a very hot oven (475 degrees) and bake for 20 minutes, or until a knife inserted comes out clean. Serve while hot.

Edward Winslow came to America from Holland on the Mayflower in 1620. He soon won the respect of the Indians when he offered himself as a hostage at the first conference between the English and the natives. He later brought the first cows and a bull to the colonies. He succeeded Bradford as governor in 1633 and remained in office for three consecutive terms. Winslow died in 1665 while at sea.

When this dish was served, Winslow liked to eat it with some fried green tomatoes or a nice green salad.

John Endicott's Savory Cheese Pudding Dinner

2 cups cheese, grated
1 teaspoon flour
1/2 teaspoon salt
1/4 teaspoon pepper
1 cup milk, boiling

1 tablespoon butter, melted
2 eggs, separated
1/2 teaspoon baking powder
2 tablespoons bread crumbs

Put the cheese into a large wooden mixing bowl and stir in the flour, salt, pepper, boiling milk and melted butter. Set aside while you beat the egg yolks slightly. Then, in a separate bowl, beat the egg whites with the baking powder until you have a stiff froth. Add both the egg yolks and the egg whites to the previous mixture. Lastly, stir in the bread crumbs. Continue to gently stir until everything is blended. Pour into a greased baking pan and bake in a moderate oven (350 degrees) for 20 minutes. Serve while hot. This recipe serves 6 people.

John Endicott was the first governor of the Massachusetts colony, but was succeeded by John Winthrop. He was again the governor in 1665 when he died in office. During his administration four Quakers were hanged in Boston.

JOHN ENDICOTT.

Colonial Potato Pot Soup—A Sullivan Treat

JOHN SULLIVAN.

1 slice bacon, cut up
1 cup beef, cooked and cut up
1 small onion, chopped
1 bay leaf

1 sprig parsley
2 large potatoes, diced
1 teaspoon salt
1/2 teaspoon pepper

Put the bacon pieces into a cast iron skillet and fry until there is plenty of grease. Add the beef pieces and the chopped onion. Stir and fry until everything has browned nicely. Dump these ingredients into a soup kettle with 6 cups cold water. Add the bay leaf and parsley. Simmer gently for 1 hour. Strain and then add the potatoes to the liquid. Allow to boil for 10 minutes. Season with the salt and pepper. Serve while hot.

John Sullivan was born in Berwick, Maine, in 1740. He was an earnest patriot and a member of the first Continental Congress.

Beef Steak as Fixed for Jonathan Trumbull

1 large steak, 1 inch thick
1 clove garlic, cut in half
1/4 cup butter
1 teaspoon salt

1 teaspoon pepper
3 tablespoons catsup
2 tablespoons Worcestershire sauce
1/2 cup coffee

Carefully rub the steak with garlic. Heat a cast iron skillet very hot and add the butter. When melted, place the steak in the skillet. Immediately turn the steak. Place skillet on rack in the oven and broil for 9 minutes. Then sprinkle some of the salt and pepper on this. Turn the steak and broil the other side for another 9 minutes. Salt and pepper it with the remaining seasoning. Take the steak from the pan and put it on a hot platter. Meanwhile, add the catsup, Worcestershire sauce and coffee to the skillet. Blend well while heating thoroughly. Pour this over the steak and serve immediately. This should feed 4 to 6 people.

Jonathan Trumbull was the only colonial governor who espoused the cause of the people in their struggle for justice and freedom. He was chosen as governor of Connecticut in 1769, after boldly refusing to take an oath required by all officers of the crown. This great man died in Lebanon, Connecticut on August 17, 1785.

John Campbell Loudoun's Apple Pudding

Loudoun was born in Scotland in 1705. He was appointed governor of the Virginia colony, and was commander-in-chief of the British forces in America in 1756. He was recalled to England in 1757 because of indecision and inefficiency. As we can see with his recipe, Loudoun was much more of a poet than an administrator:

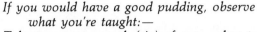

*If you would have a good pudding, observe
    what you're taught:—
Take two pennyworth (six) of eggs, when twelve
    for the groat (fourpence):
And of the same fruit that Eve had once
    chosen,
Well pared and well chopp'd, at least
    half-a-dozen;
Six ounces of bread, let your maid eat
    the crust,
The crumbs must be grated as small as
    the dust;
Six ounces of currants from the stones
    you must sort,
Lest they brake out your teeth, and spoil
    all your sport;
Five ounces of sugar won't make it
    too sweet;
Some salt and some nutmegg will make
    it compleat,
Three hours let it boyle, without hurry
    or flutter,
And then serve it up without sugar
    or butter.*

Favorites of American Patriots

One of our nicest traditions is fondness for nostalgia in the kitchen. Many worthwhile recipes will never be forgotten or lost, thanks to the innumerable old recipe compilers who have recorded for posterity the favorite dishes of so many famous people of the past. For example, Davy Crockett, who was killed at the Alamo in 1836, actually enjoyed eating rawhide when other food wasn't readily available. He said to fix it this way: "Scorch and scrape the hair off. This has a tendency to kill and purify the bad taste that scalding gave it. After scraping, boil one hour, throwing the water away that had extracted all the glue, then wash and let it get cold, and then eat with a little sugar sprinkled on it."

William Ellery, a signer of the Declaration of Independence, often enjoyed a bread pudding he called, "Spotted Dog," because of the raisins it contained. And

Thomas Paine dearly loved "Red Flannel Hash" which was made with the unlikely combination of beets, potatoes, onion and beef.

Count de Rochambeau's Stewed Mushrooms
Gather together grown mushrooms, but such as are young enough to have red gills; cut off that part of the stem which grew in the earth—wash them carefully, and take the skin from the top; put them into a stew pan with some salt, but no water—stew them till tender, and thicken them with a spoonful of butter, mixed with one of brown flour; some cream and eggs; red wine may be added, but the flavour of the mushroom is too delicious to require aid from any thing.

Count De Rochambeau's Stewed Mushrooms

Method 1
1 cup mushrooms
1/2 teaspoon salt
1 tablespoon butter
1 tablespoon flour
1 egg
3 tablespoons cream

Method 2
1 cup mushrooms
1 cup milk, warm
1/2 teaspoon salt
1/2 teaspoon pepper
1/4 cup butter, melted
1 tablespoon flour, wet in
    cold milk
1 egg, well beaten

Put the mushrooms into a porcelain saucepan and cover them with cold water. Bring to a boil and then stir gently for 15 minutes while simmering. Add the salt. Chop the butter into bits and roll in flour. Add this to the mushrooms and boil for 4 minutes, stirring continuously. Now whip the egg and cream together. Put this mixture with the mushrooms and stir for 2 minutes without letting it boil.

Put the mushrooms into a porcelain saucepan and cover them with cold water. Bring to a boil and then stew gently for 10 minutes. Now strain off the water and add the warm milk in its place. Simmer this for 5 minutes more. Add the salt, pepper and melted butter. Thicken it with the wet flour and the frothy beaten egg. Pour into a bowl and serve immediately.

General Jean Rochambeau (1725-1807) teamed up with Washington and DeGrasse to defeat Cornwallis at the siege of Yorktown on October 19, 1781. He came to America with 6,000 men to aid the patriot cause in 1770. (General Rochambeau preferred the second method of preparation over the first.)

Walnut Gypsy Stew—A Favorite of Anthony Wayne

2 tablespoons butter
1 pound veal, ground
2 tablespoons flour
1 cup milk

3 tablespoons cheese, grated
3/4 teaspoon salt
1/2 teaspoon pepper
3 tablespoons walnuts, chopped

Put the butter into a cast iron skillet and let it melt. Fry the ground veal until it is done. Stir in the flour and blend well. Now add the milk and stir as it heats. Add the cheese, stirring thoroughly until it is all melted. Lastly, blend in the salt, pepper and chopped walnuts. Serve while very hot.

General Anthony Wayne (1745-96) was quoted as saying he never tired of this stew. He was a famous commander during the Revolutionary War who raised a volunteer regiment in 1776. This man was a hero of the storming and capture of Stony Point on July 15, 1779. He became known as "Mad Anthony," and stopped Indian uprisings in the West of 1794.

GEN. WAYNE

John Paul Jones Special Cauliflower Dish

1 head cauliflower, large
1 onion, large
1 bunch celery
3/4 cup cream

3 tablespoons butter
1 teaspoon salt
1 teaspoon pepper
1/2 teaspoon mace

Put the head of cauliflower into a large cast iron pot and cover with cold salted water. Bring to a boil and cook until about half done. Then change the water and throw it away. Again cover the cauliflower with fresh salted water and bring to a boil. Allow this to simmer until tender. Drain the cauliflower and set aside 3/4 cup of the cooking water. Chop up the cauliflower and set it aside. Now put the onion and celery into the empty kettle and cover with water. Bring to a boil and cook until tender. When done, drain and then chop them up together. Set this aside. Put the 3/4 cup of cauliflower water into the kettle and simmer. Stir in the cream. Add the cooked cauliflower, onion and celery. Chop up the butter and roll the bits in flour. Add this and the seasonings to the mixture. Bring to a quick boil and allow it to simmer until thickened. Serve immediately.

John Paul Jones developed a taste for this delicious dish while engaged in the African slave trade between 1766 and 1767, under his real name of John Paul. He assumed the name *Jones* when later relocating in Virginia. This man became well-known as an American naval officer at the outbreak of the Revolutionary War. He later saw service as a rear admiral in the Russian navy of 1788.

Muhlenberg's Stewed Apple Coffeecake

1 cup dried apples,
    chopped fine
1 cup molasses or
1 cup honey
1 cup sugar
1/2 cup butter
2 eggs
1/2 cup sour milk or
1/2 cup coffee
1 teaspoon baking soda
1 teaspoon cloves
1 teaspoon cinnamon
1 teaspoon allspice
1 1/2 cups flour

Put the dried apples into a saucepan with a little water and allow them to stew for 10 minutes. Then add the molasses or honey and simmer for 1 full hour. When done, set aside to cool. Meanwhile take a large wooden mixing bowl and cream the sugar with the butter. Beat in the eggs, sour milk or coffee, baking soda and spices. When the apple mixture has cooled to lukewarm stir it in with these ingredients. Lastly work in the flour to make a stiff batter. Put this batter into a well-buttered and floured shallow baking pan. Bake in a very slow oven (275 degrees) for 1 hour.

This old German recipe was concocted by the Muhlenberg family many years ago. John (1746-1807) was a general during the Revolutionary War. He was commander-in-chief in Virginia until the arrival of Steuben, and later served as a member of Congress between 1789 and 1801.

Timothy Pickering's Pumpkin Custard

1 cup pumpkin, stewed and mashed
3 eggs, well beaten
3/4 cup brown sugar
1/2 teaspoon salt

1/8 teaspoon nutmeg
1/2 teaspoon cinnamon
2 cups milk, scalding
1 cup cream, whipped

Put the stewed pumpkin into a wooden mixing bowl and blend in the frothy beaten eggs, brown sugar, salt and spices. When well mixed stir in the hot milk. Beat the mixture hard and thoroughly. Pour the custard into a buttered baking pan or 6 custard cups. Set in a shallow pan of hot water and bake in a moderately hot oven (375 degrees) for 25 to 30 minutes, or until firm. Set aside to cool. Serve when cold with the whipped cream on top.

This wonderful old-time pumpkin dish originated with the Pickering family. The first armed resistance to British troops was led by Timothy Pickering, as colonel of the militia, in February, 1775, at a drawbridge in Salem. In the fall of 1776, Pickering joined Washington in New Jersey, with his regiment of 700 men.

Sour Cream Salad Dressing Enjoyed by Robert Morris

1 cup sour cream
3 egg yolks, well beaten
1 teaspoon mustard
1/2 tablespoon olive oil

1/4 teaspoon salt
1/8 teaspoon pepper
1/4 cup cider vinegar

ROBERT MORRIS.

Pour the sour cream into a double boiler and bring to a good boil. Pour this into the custard-like beaten egg yolks. Stir in the mustard, salt and pepper. Put back into the double boiler and cook until it thickens. Stir frequently to stop from sticking and burning. Take from the stove and set aside to cool. When cold, stir in the cider vinegar and the olive oil.

This particular salad dressing has great historical significance. It was a lifelong favorite of Robert Morris (1734-1806) who was known as the "Financier of the American Revolution." This great man was a member of the Continental Congress in 1776 and bravely signed the Declaration of Independence.

General Lafayette's Favorite Herb Omelette

6 eggs, separated
1 cup cream
1/2 teaspoon salt
1/2 teaspoon pepper

2 tablespoons parsley
2 tablespoons thyme
2 tablespoons marjoram
2 tablespoons onion, minced

Beat the egg yolks in a wooden mixing bowl until they are smooth and thick. Stir in the cream, salt and pepper. Now beat the egg whites until they will stand alone. Lightly fold whites into the previous mixture. When the omelet is ready to be poured into a hot buttered cast iron skillet stir in the herbs and the onion. Pour into the skillet. Cook for 10 minutes. Do not stir, but slip a broad-bladed knife under the omelet to guard against burning on the bottom. As soon as the middle of the omelet has "set," place the skillet in a hot oven (425 degrees) and let it bake for 10 minutes. When done, lay a hot dish bottom upward on top of the skillet. Turn the skillet over on the dish to bring the browned side of the omelet uppermost. Eat immediately as it will soon fall.

Great-Great-Grandmother Huldah Horton fixed this dish at the request of General Lafayette when he visited her home in Newburgh, New York, in 1824, on his last visit to America.

Green Corn Pudding Specialty of Ethan Allen

12 large ears corn
5 egg yolks, well beaten
2 tablespoons butter,
    melted
1 tablespoon sugar

1/4 teaspoon salt
4 cups cream or
4 cups milk
5 egg whites, stiffly beaten

Grate the raw corn from the cobs and put in a large wooden mixing bowl. Stir in the custard-like egg yolks and beat it together *very* hard. Stir in the melted butter, sugar and salt. Gradually add the cream or milk, beating hard all the time. Lastly fold in the fluffy beaten egg whites and pour into a deep buttered baking pan. Cover and bake in a moderate oven (350 degrees) for 1 hour. Then remove the cover and continue baking until the top of the pudding is nicely browned.

This, according to Ethan Allen, "is a most delicious dish when properly mixed and baked." He liked what was left over from dinner as a breakfast treat. He would moisten it with a little warm milk and then stir it in a skillet until smoking hot. Green corn pudding was extremely popular in the Colonies before the American Revolution. Ethan Allen (1737-89) was leader of the famed Green Mountain Boys. This man's name became a household word when he daringly stormed and captured Fort Ticonderoga in 1775. Allen forced the commander to surrender "in the name of the Great Jehovah and Continental Congress."

ETHAN ALLEN.

Richard Henry Lee's Stuffed Meat Loaf

1 1/2 pounds beef, ground
1/2 pound pork, ground
4 slices bread, soaked in milk, drained
1 onion, chopped fine
1 tablespoon salt
1/2 teaspoon pepper
2 eggs

Combine all the above ingredients in a large wooden mixing bowl. Blend thoroughly and using 2/3 of the mixture, line the bottom and sides of a loaf pan. Set aside and make the stuffing as follows:

1/4 cup butter
3 onions, chopped fine
2 stalks celery, chopped fine
1 1/2 cups soft bread crumbs
1/2 teaspoon sage

1/2 teaspoon salt
1/8 teaspoon pepper
2 tablespoons parsley
2 tablespoons water
1 egg, well beaten

Melt the butter in a cast iron skillet. Put in the onion and the celery and fry until the onions are transparent. Stir in the bread crumbs, sage, salt, pepper, parsley and water. Sauté until slightly browned. Remove from the stove and stir in the beaten egg. Fill center portion of meat covered loaf pan with this stuffing. Cover the top with the remaining 1/3 of the meat mixture. Then to complete this tasty dish, you will need:

2 tablespoons butter, melted
1/2 cup water
1/2 cup chili sauce

Spread the top of the loaf with melted butter. Pour the water over this and cover with chili sauce. Bake in a moderate oven (350 degrees) for 45 minutes. This recipe serves 6 to 8 people. The Lee family enjoyed this dish when accompanied with baked potatoes and a green salad.

Richard Henry Lee was a general during the Revolutionary War and was best known as "Lighthorse Harry." He served as governor of Virginia from 1792 to 1795. Lee was a close personal friend of Washington and delivered the funeral oration when George died. It contained those now famous words: "First in war, first in peace, first in the hearts of his countrymen."

Israel Putnam's Baked Ham and Apples

2 large slices ham,
    1/3 inch thick
2 teaspoons mustard
2 tablespoons vinegar
2 cooking apples, sliced thin
1/2 cup brown sugar

Remove the bone from the ham slices. Mix together the mustard and the vinegar in a small wooden mixing bowl. Spread this thickly over the slices of ham. Lay the apple slices on the ham. Sprinkle well with brown sugar. Now roll the ham slices the long way, starting from the fatty side and rolling the fat into the center. Hold together with tooth picks. Place in a greased baking pan and lay a few dabs of butter on each ham roll. Bake in a hot oven (425 degrees) for 30 minutes. Baste twice with butter while baking. Serve while hot.

General Israel Putnam (1718-90) was in charge of defending Philadelphia during the Revolutionary War. He was also prominent at the battle of Bunker Hill in 1775. Putnam's mother was said to have first concocted this delightfully simple but tasty ham dish.

ISRAEL PUTNAM IN 1776.

RICHARD HENRY LEE.

General Horatio Gates' Best Rice Popovers

Put the cooked rice into a wooden mixing bowl and mash until smooth. In another bowl sift together the flour, baking powder, sugar and salt. Sift twice. Beat the egg yolks until creamy and the egg whites until they are a stiff froth. Blend the egg yolks and whites together and stir them into the rice. Then add the cream and flour alternately, and beat until smooth. Butter some gem pans and sift a little flour into each. Fill each 2/3 full with the mixture. Bake in a hot oven (425 degrees) for 15 minutes. Serve while hot with butter and maple syrup. This recipe makes 20 popovers.

General Horatio Gates (1728-1806) had a special love for rice popovers made in this manner. As an American general during the Revolutionary War, he defeated British troops under General Burgoyne at Saratoga on October 17, 1777.

1 cup boiled rice, cold
2 cups flour
2 teaspoons baking powder
2 tablespoons sugar
1 teaspoon salt
2 eggs, separated
2 cups cream

Iron Gem Pans

John P. Schuyler's Corn Relish

*1 large head cabbage,
    chopped fine
2 tablespoons salt
12 ears of corn
4 large onions, chopped fine
2 red peppers, chopped fine*

Put the cabbage into a large cast iron pot and sprinkle with salt. Set aside and let stand for 1 hour. Meanwhile boil the ears of corn. When cooked, cut from the cob. Add the onions and peppers to the corn. Drain the cabbage. Now add the corn, onions and pepper to this. Set aside while making the sauce as follows:

*6 cups vinegar
1 tablespoon mustard
2 teaspoons salt
1 tablespoon celery seeds
1 cup sugar
1 tablespoon flour
1 teaspoon tumeric*

Blend the vinegar, mustard, salt, celery seeds and sugar in a wooden mixing bowl. Pour this over the mixture in the cast iron pot. Let it all come to a boil.

Blend the flour with the tumeric and add it to the boiling pot. Cook for 10 minutes and seal in sterile jars.

This very old recipe dates back to Colonial times and the family of John Philip Schuyler (1733-1804). He served as a Captain in the British army during the French and Indian War in 1756. This famous man was a member of the Colonial Assembly in 1768 and a delegate to the Continental Congress in 1775.

PHILIP (JOHN) SCHUYLER.

The dining room in the Nathan Hale homestead, Coventry, Connecticut. The rifle over the fireplace was Nathan's boyhood fowl gun. He often used it for hunting wild game.

The Jefferson Family

Thomas Jefferson's early American recipes are thought to be much like Lot's wife. They all look back over their shoulders. Unlike the lady who turned into salt, they are thought by many not to be looking back upon Sodom, but upon paradise.

Jefferson was known widely as a gourmet food buff. His slaves had brought over with them some unique "benne" seeds. He made a salad oil from them and considered it to be the equal of olive oil. He even edged his flower beds with these plants. Today we know the "benne" seeds as sesame seeds.

This great man was also a great connoisseur of wine. He spent untold hours writing copious notes on wines between 1784 and 1789 and sent them to George Washington. He offered: "A general observation as to all wines is that there is great differences in those of the same vineyard in different years, and this affects the price considerably."

One of Jefferson's favorite holiday drinks was "A Yard of Flannel." It was simply a mixture of hot ale combined with eggs, sugar, nutmeg and dark rum.

Thomas Jefferson's Simple Bread Pudding
Grate the crumb of a stale loaf, and pour on it a pint of boiling milk—let it stand an hour, then beat it to a pulp; add six eggs, well beaten, half a pound of butter, the same of powdered sugar, half a nutmeg, a glass of brandy, and some grated lemon peel—put a paste in the dish, and bake it.

Thomas Jefferson's Simple Bread Pudding

MONTICELLO.

Add the bread crumbs to the scalded milk in a large wooden mixing bowl. Then stir in the brandy, sugar and melted butter. Set aside and allow to cool. When cold, add the beaten eggs. Lastly, stir in the nutmeg and lemon peel. Pour into custard cups and place in a pan half full of water. Bake in a moderate oven (350 degrees) for 45 minutes or until a knife inserted comes out dry. Thomas Jefferson especially enjoyed this pudding with a chocolate sauce. He made it as follows:

3/4 cup sugar
1 tablespoon flour
1 square chocolate, melted
1/2 cup water

Blend the sugar with the flour. Then add the melted chocolate and the water. Stir while boiling for 5 minutes and serve.

1 cup bread crumbs
2 cups milk, scalded
1/4 cup brandy
1/2 cup sugar
1 tablespoon butter, melted
2 eggs, beaten
1/2 teaspoon nutmeg
1/2 teaspoon lemon peel, grated

French Chicken Kiev

1/2 cup butter
1 tablespoon chives
1 tablespoon lemon juice
4 chicken breasts, boned
4 teaspoons salt
2 teaspoons pepper
3 eggs, well beaten
1/4 cup water
2 cups bread crumbs, fine

Take a small wooden bowl and blend together the butter, chives and lemon juice. Chill until hardened. Halve the chicken breasts and remove the skin. Cut through the thickest section of each half-breast to form a pocket. Sprinkle each half breast with salt and pepper. Place 1 tablespoon of the chilled chive butter in each pocket. Set aside and blend the eggs and water in a wooden mixing bowl. Dip the chicken breasts in the egg mixture. Roll in bread crumbs. Dip each chicken breast a second time. Again roll in bread crumbs. Set aside to chill for 1 hour. Deep fry in hot (350 degrees) cooking oil for 10 minutes. Serve immediately.

Jefferson's Chops and Potato Casserole

1 pound pork chops
6 sweet potatoes, sliced
2 medium onions, sliced
3 tablespoons flour
2 teaspoons salt
2 teaspoons pepper

Cut the pork chops into small pieces. Put a layer on the bottom of a buttered baking pan. Follow this with a layer of sweet potatoes and a layer of onions. Sprinkle this layer with some of the flour, salt and pepper. Continue making layers with the pork, sweet potatoes and onions until the ingredients are all used. Cover with cold water and bake in a moderate oven (350 degrees) for 2 hours. This recipe is enough to serve 5 people.

Jefferson's Favorite Horseradish Vinegar

4 cups vinegar
1 tablespoon sugar
6 tablespoons horseradish,
    scraped or grated

Put the vinegar and sugar into a saucepan and stir until the sugar has all dissolved. Bring to a boil and pour over the horseradish. Put this mixture into a good stone jar, cover tightly, and let it steep for 1 week. Immediately strain and put into sterile bottles.

Thomas Jefferson preferred the taste of this vinegar over all others, and he was known to make his own batch when the supply ran low.

Mrs. Jefferson's Egg and Tomato Bake

3 large tomatoes
3 eggs
1 teaspoon salt
1/2 teaspoon pepper
3 tablespoons bread crumbs
1 tablespoon butter
3 slices bacon, cut in half

Scoop out the centers of the large ripe tomatoes. Break one egg carefully into each tomato and sprinkle each with some of the salt and pepper. Fry the bread crumbs in the butter and put this mixture over the eggs in the tomatoes. Lay 2 small slices of the bacon over each tomato. Bake in a moderate oven (350 degrees) for 30 minutes. Turn the bacon once during baking. Place under the broiler for 1 minute to crisp and brown the bacon. Serve while very hot.

Jefferson's Favorite French Custard

1/2 cup sugar
1 1/2 tablespoons flour
1 1/2 tablespoons cornstarch
1/4 teaspoon salt
2 1/4 cups cream or
2 1/4 cups milk
1 egg, well beaten
1 1/2 teaspoons vanilla
3/4 cup cream, whipped

Combine the sugar, flour, cornstarch and salt in a saucepan. Gradually stir in the cream or milk. Cook, stirring constantly, until mixture comes to a boil and thickens. Cook for 3 more minutes, always stirring. Take a little of the hot mixture out of the saucepan and stir it into the beaten egg. Then add this to the hot mixture in the pan. Allow to cook 1 minute. Take from the stove and add the vanilla. Beat until smooth and creamy. Lastly, fold in the whipped cream. Set aside to cool and then serve. This makes 3 nice cups. Jefferson enjoyed this custard so much that he often ate all of it himself. He even loved it hot.

Martha Jefferson's Chicken Pudding

2 chickens, 3 pounds each
1/2 cup butter
3 teaspoons salt
2 teaspoons pepper
1 teaspoon garlic powder

Wash, cut up and skin the chickens. Put the pieces into a large kettle with the butter and enough water to cover. Season with the salt, pepper and garlic powder. Bring this to a boil and then allow to stew slowly for 30 minutes. Then take the chicken out of the kettle and lay the pieces on a platter to cool. Set aside the water in which the chicken was stewed. This will later be used for gravy. Now make a batter by blending the following ingredients:

4 cups milk
3 cups flour
3 tablespoons butter, melted
4 eggs, well beaten
1/4 teaspoon salt
1/8 teaspoon pepper
1 teaspoon cream of tartar

Put a layer of the chicken pieces in the bottom of a large buttered baking pan. Pour 1/2 cup of the batter over this. Add another layer of chicken, and more of the batter. Continue until all of the chicken is used. Take whatever is left of the batter and pour it over the top as a crust. Bake in a moderate oven (350 degrees) for 1 hour. While the chicken is baking, prepare the gravy as follows:

1 egg, well beaten
2 teaspoons flour
1 teaspoon parsley

Put the beaten egg in the stew water set aside previously. Stir well and slowly add the flour until it thickens. Then stir in the parsley. Bring to a quick boil and pour into a gravy boat. Serve portions of the baked chicken dish with a little gravy on top. Thomas Jefferson believed this to be the finest chicken dish ever made by his wife.

Jefferson's Favorite Sugarless Corn Bread

1 cup corn meal
1 cup flour
2 teaspoons baking powder
1/2 teaspoon salt
2 eggs, separated
3 cups cream or
3 cups milk
2 tablespoons butter, melted

Sift the corn meal, flour, baking powder and salt into a large wooden mixing bowl. Beat the egg yolks in another bowl and add 2 cups of the cream or milk to them. Then stir in the melted butter. When well blended, add this smooth batter to the flour mixture in the wooden bowl. Stir until everything is completely blended. Beat the egg whites to a stiff froth and fold them into the other ingredients. Pour into a square baking pan that has been well buttered. The batter should be about 2 inches thick. Lastly, pour into the middle the remaining cup of cream or milk. Do not stir. Place very gently into a moderate oven (350 degrees) and bake for 50 minutes. Turn out, cut in squares and serve while hot. The center of this delightful dish will be a custard. This recipe is enough for 6 people.

Tomato Cocktail—
Martha's Specialty Drink

4 quarts tomatoes, crushed
2 medium onions, minced
2 green peppers, minced
2 stalks celery, minced
2 teaspoons salt
2 teaspoons sugar
2 bay leaves
1 cup water, hot

Blend all of the above ingredients in a large cast iron kettle. Bring to a boil and allow to simmer for 1 1/2 hours. Take out the bay leaves and rub the rest of the mixture through a sieve three times. Then pour into jars or bottles and seal until ready to use. Chill and serve.

Cutlets A La Thomas Jefferson

2 onions, chopped
1 1/2 cups bacon grease
1 1/2 pounds veal cutlets
2 large tomatoes
2 cups milk
2 teaspoons salt
1 teaspoon pepper

Put the chopped onions into a cast iron skillet with the bacon grease. Fry until the onions turn yellow. Add the veal cutlets and partially cook them. Crush the tomatoes to a pulp and add to the skillet. Stir in the milk, salt and pepper. Cook for another 10 minutes. Remove the veal cutlets and place them on a large platter. Continue cooking the sauce in the skillet until it thickens. Then pour the sauce over the cutlets and serve while hot. This recipe serves 6 people.

Jefferson Squash Doughnuts

2 tablespoons butter
1 1/4 cups sugar
2 eggs, well beaten
1 cup squash, cooked
1 teaspoon vanilla
3 cups flour
1/2 teaspoon salt
3 teaspoons baking powder
1/2 teaspoon cinnamon
1/2 teaspoon nutmeg
1 cup milk

Cream the butter and sugar in a large wooden mixing bowl. Then stir in the eggs, squash and vanilla. Sift the flour with salt, baking powder, cinnamon and nutmeg. Add this alternately with the milk to the first mixture. Blend well and set aside to chill. When the dough is cold, turn it out on a lightly floured surface. Roll out to a 1/3 inch thick sheet. Cut with a floured cutter and deep fry in hot grease until brown. Drain on absorbent paper or cloth before serving.

Apple Catsup—
A Jefferson Family Favorite

4 cups apple sauce, unsweetened
1 teaspoon ginger
1 teaspoon cinnamon
1 teaspoon cloves
1 teaspoon mustard
1 teaspoon onion juice
2 teaspoons salt
1 teaspoon pepper
2 cups vinegar

Combine all of the above ingredients in a large saucepan. Bring to a boil and allow to simmer slowly until it thickens. Bottle, or put into sterile jars and seal until needed.

Rule for Proper Steak Cookery

These are the rules adopted by the celebrated Beefsteak Club of 1734 England. This was highly recommended by Jefferson as the only way to really cook a steak:

Pound well your meat till the fibres break,
Be sure that next you have, to broil the steak,
Good coal in plenty; nor a moment leave,
But turn it over this way, and then that;
The lean should be quite rare—not so the fat.
The platter now and then the juice receive,
Put on your butter, place it on your meat,
Salt, Pepper, turn it over, serve, and eat.

The First First Lady—Martha Washington

Many of the following recipes are credited to Martha Washington, although she didn't actually compile them. This was done by her mother-in-law (mother of Martha's first husband, Daniel Custis), Frances Parke Custis. Mrs. Custis gave her personal small cookery guide to Martha, who after many years of using it, handed the book down to her beloved granddaughter, Nellie Custis.

This leather-bound book is divided into two major sections. The first, "A Booke of Cookery," has 206 handwritten entries. The second section, "A Booke of Sweetmeats," contains 326 handwritten recipes. Each section also includes a neatly arranged table of contents.

The book's inscription reads: "This book, written by Eleanor Parke Custis's great grandmother, Mrs. John Custis, was given to her, by her beloved Grandmother Martha Washington—formerly Mrs. Daniel Custis."

Other recipes are credited directly to Martha Washington, as they come from her own personal *Rules for Cooking.* This book is legible, neatly compiled group of recipes Martha collected over the years, as she, Mrs. Thomas Jefferson, Mrs. James Monroe, and other lady friends exchanged their best recipes among themselves. Martha eventually had over 500 of her favorite recipes in this collection. The first recipe given in this chapter is exactly as originally written, followed by an updated version for today's homemaker. The balance of the recipes have all been rewritten for modern cooking.

To Make Exolent Pan Cakes

  Take eggs, beat them very well, put to them a quart of Cream & as much flower as is needfull, then put in a pd of frefs Butter, & a grated Nutmegg & Salt, and let it Stand where it may keep warm but not too hott, so frye it in a fine frying pan without butter.

Residence of George Washington at
Mount Vernon.

To Make Excellent Pancakes

3 cups flour
3 1/2 teaspoons baking powder
3/4 teaspoon salt

1/2 teaspoon nutmeg
3/4 cups butter
3 egg yolks, well beaten
2 cups cream or
2 cups milk
3 egg whites, stiffly beaten

Sift the flour, baking powder, salt and nutmeg into a large wooden mixing bowl. Cut in the butter with a fork until the resulting mixture is as fine as corn meal. Combine the beaten egg yolks and the cream or milk in a separate bowl. Add this to the flour mixture and beat until the batter is smooth. Lastly, fold in the beaten egg whites. Turn the batter into a wide-mouthed pitcher and pour onto a hot, well greased griddle. Each pancake should be about the size of a saucer. When nicely browned on one side, turn with a spatula. When nicely browned on the other side, remove from the griddle and place on a warm dish. These griddle cakes should be served hot with butter and maple syrup, or with sugar and milk, both of which Martha and George thoroughly enjoyed as a breakfast dish. Note: Martha would sometimes vary this recipe by adding 1 cup cooked ham or 1 cup grated cheese to her batter before cooking. This recipe makes about 25 pancakes.

Mary Washington's Oyster Sauce for Roast Chicken

24 oysters, in shell
1 large onion, minced
1/8 teaspoon mace
1 teaspoon salt
1/2 teaspoon pepper
1/2 lemon, juice only
1 tablespoon butter, well
    rounded
1/2 cup bread crumbs
1/2 cup wine

Open the oysters over a saucepan and save the liquor. Set the oysters aside in a wooden mixing bowl while preparing the gravy sauce. To the oyster liquor add the minced onion and the mace. Simmer slowly and stir until the onion is cooked. Then stir in the salt, pepper, lemon juice and butter. Stir continuously until the butter has all melted. Lastly, blend in the bread crumbs, wine and oysters. Allow to simmer until the edges of the oysters curl. Serve immediately, while hot, by pouring this over the roast chicken. This dish was a specialty of Mary Washington, who was George's mother. She sometimes made it for George and Martha when they visited.

English Plum Pudding—A Favorite of Nellie Custis

2 cups flour
5 teaspoons baking powder
1 teaspoon salt
1 tablespoon cinnamon
1 tablespoon ginger
2 tablespoons nutmeg
2 2/3 cups brown sugar
2 cups bread crumbs
1 cup blanched almonds,
    chopped
4 cups suet, chopped
4 cups currants

2 cups black raisins
2 cups yellow raisins
2 cups cherries, halved
4 cups figs, chopped
4 cups apples, peeled
    and diced
2 orange rinds, grated
2 lemon rinds, grated
10 eggs, well beaten
1 cup brandy
2 tablespoons butter,
    melted

Blend the flour, baking powder, salt and spices in a large wooden mixing bowl. Then stir in the brown sugar. When well mixed, add the bread crumbs, almonds and suet. Stir and add the various fruits, including the orange and lemon rinds. In a separate bowl, blend the beaten eggs, brandy and melted butter. Add this mixture to that in the first bowl and blend thoroughly. Add a little more brandy if necessary to make a stiff dough. Allow to stand in a cool place for 1 hour. Then divide the dough and put it into two well-greased molds. Cover and steam steadily for 10 hours. This pudding should be kept in a cool place for at least 1 week before eating. Before serving, steam for a couple hours. This recipe is sufficient for 12 to 14 persons. George Washington often enjoyed leftover cold plum pudding when it was sliced and fried. Plum pudding is wonderful when served with whipped cream, or with foamy sauce, a Washington Specialty. It is made as follows:

6 tablespoons butter
1 cup powdered sugar
3 eggs, separated
1 teaspoon vanilla
2 tablespoons water, boiling

Cream the butter and add the sugar slowly while continuously beating. In separate bowls, beat the egg yolks until thick and the egg whites until stiff. Then gradually add the egg yolks to the butter-sugar mixture and beat well. Add the stiffly beaten egg whites, the vanilla and boiling water. Stir until all ingredients are blended nicely. Before serving, heat over boiling water, stirring constantly.

Martha's Special Ham and Parsnips

1 1/2 pounds ham, cut in 1 inch slices
6 cloves, whole
1 tablespoon nutmeg
1/4 cup water
1/2 cup honey
2 cups parsnips, sliced and cooked

Place the slices of ham in a baking pan. Stick cloves in the ham and sprinkle the slices with nutmeg. Add the water and honey. Cover and bake in a moderately slow oven (325 degrees) for 45 minutes. Remove from the oven and cover the ham with parsnips. Return the baking pan, uncovered, to the oven and bake until nicely browned. Martha sometimes used sweet potatoes in place of parsnips. It's delicious either way. This recipe serves 6 people.

George Washington's Favorite Pumpkin Pie

3/4 cup sugar
1 teaspoon cinnamon
1 teaspoon ginger
1/2 teaspoon salt
1 1/2 cups pumpkin, steamed
   and strained
3 eggs, beaten
1 1/2 cups milk
1/2 cup cream
1 tablespoon butter, melted

Put the sugar into a large wooden mixing bowl and blend in the cinnamon, ginger and salt. Then stir in the pumpkin, beaten eggs, milk, cream and butter. Blend well and pour into a pastry lined pie pan. Bake in a moderate oven (350 degrees) for 45 minutes. Allow to cool and then serve. Sufficient for one pie.

George and Martha's Favorite Mince Meat

Cook the ground beef and after it cools, add all of the above ingredients. Be sure to blend all of this thoroughly. Set aside and get a large saucepan. Boil together these ingredients:

1 quart apple cider
1 quart brandy
2 tablespoons butter

Pour this mixture over the other ingredients in the bowl. When cool, pack in jars, or simply cover the bowl well, and store in a cold, dry place. Allow to stand for at least 24 hours before using for pies. This amount of mince meat will make from 8 to 12 delicious pies. Mince meat made in this way will stay good for more than 6 months. George Washington had a definite weakness for pies of this kind. Martha found it well worthwhile making up a large batch, for if planned wisely, it only had to be undertaken once each winter. But, she recommended not eating these pies at night before going to bed if the eater valued his own sound slumber.

5 pounds beef, ground
1 pound beef suet, ground
2 pounds raisins
2 pounds currants
1 tablespoon cloves
2 tablespoons cinnamon
1 tablespoon ginger

1 tablespoon nutmeg
1/2 tablespoon salt
1/2 teaspoon pepper
4 cups sugar
1 lemon, juice and rind
1/2 pound citron peel
8 cups apples, chopped fine

Yorkshire Country Captain—Eaten by Charles Peale

1 chicken, three pounds
Salt to suit
Pepper to suit
Curry powder to suit
Flour to suit
1/4 cup onion, minced
3/4 cup salt pork, minced

2 cups chicken stock
2 tablespoons butter
2 tablespoons flour
3 large onions, thinly sliced and fried
24 almonds, toasted in butter
2 cups peas, cooked
3/4 cup rice, steamed

Cut the chicken in small pieces. Dredge each piece with salt, pepper, curry powder and flour. Fry the minced onion and the salt pork until golden brown. Add the pieces of chicken and slowly brown. When nicely browned, add the chicken stock. Cover and allow to simmer slowly until the chicken is tender. Remove the chicken from the pan. Combine the butter and flour in a small wooden mixing bowl. Add to the chicken broth to thicken. Cook, stirring constantly, until smooth. Season to taste. Arrange the pieces of chicken on a large platter and cover with the gravy. Fry the onion slices until golden brown and lay over the chicken. Sprinkle on the almonds. Lastly, add the peas and steamed rice. Serve at once. This recipe is designed to serve 6 hungry people.

Charles Wilson Peale was a portrait painter. In 1772 he painted the first portrait of George Washington ever executed, in the costume of a Virginia colonel. At the same time he painted a miniature of Martha.

CHARLES WILSON PEALE.

Lamb Casserole—
A George Washington Favorite

8 large potatoes, sliced
8 lamb chops
Salt to suit
Pepper to suit
8 onions, sliced

Take a large stewing pan and carefully put in a layer of raw potatoes. Then follow with a layer of lamb chops. Sprinkle this liberally with salt and pepper. Lastly, add a layer of sliced onions. Continue this sequence until all the ingredients are used up. Bake in a slow oven (300 degrees) until done, or about 1 hour. Note: This recipe can be decreased or increased, according to how many people are to be served. Simply figure 1 lamb chop, 1 potato and 1 onion per person.

Mount Vernon Cucumber Soup

3 cups cucumbers, sliced thin
4 cups chicken stock
1 slice onion
1/4 cup butter
1/4 cup flour
1 teaspoon salt
1/2 teaspoon pepper
2 cups milk, hot

Parboil the cucumber slices for 10 minutes. While doing this, put the chicken stock in a kettle and let it simmer. Drain the cucumber slices and add them to the chicken stock. Add the slice of onion. Cook until the cucumbers and onion are soft. Take out of the kettle and rub through a strainer. Put back into the chicken stock. Now blend the butter and the flour. Add this to the soup to thicken, stirring continuously. Season with the salt and pepper. Lastly, stir in the hot milk. Strain and serve while piping hot.

Martha's Most Delicious Ale Fritters

2 cups ale
1/4 cup white wine
8 egg yolks, well beaten
2 egg whites, well beaten
5 cups flour
1 teaspoon nutmeg
1/2 teaspoon cloves
1/2 teaspoon mace
8 cups apples, cut in small chunks

Blend the ale and wine in a skillet and heat until slightly warm. Set aside and put the beaten egg yolks in a large wooden mixing bowl. Add the stiff egg whites and flour. Beat these ingredients thoroughly until the batter is very thick. Then stir in the warm ale-wine mixture from the skillet. *You must not add any more flour once the ale has been added to the eggs.* Now add the various spices. The finished batter should be just thick enough to hang onto the apple pieces. Lastly, drop the pieces of apple into the batter and set aside while heating a kettle of cooking oil. When the oil is hot enough for deep frying, drop the batter by spoonfuls into the kettle. Cook until nicely browned.

Then remove each fritter from the kettle and lay on a clean cloth in a colander. Sprinkle with cinnamon and powdered sugar just before serving. George Washington liked these fritters served with maple syrup.

Veal Rice Pie Enjoyed by George and Martha

2 tablespoons salt pork, diced
1 cup potatoes, diced
1 medium onion, chopped
1/4 cup cooking oil
4 cups veal, cooked and diced
1 cup water
1 tablespoon salt
1 teaspoon pepper
1/3 cup rice, steamed
1 cup tomatoes
2 eggs, hardboiled and sliced
2 tablespoons butter

Combine the salt pork, potatoes and onion in a cast iron skillet and brown in the hot cooking oil. Stir in the veal and the water. Heat thoroughly. Season with salt and pepper. Pour this meat mixture into a well-greased baking dish and cover with rice, tomatoes and boiled egg slices. Dot the top with butter and cover the baking dish. Bake in a moderately quick oven (375 degrees) for 30 minutes. More water may be added if necessary. This recipe makes 8 nice servings.

Traditional Early New England

In early New England, electric freezers were unheard of, as were refrigerators. Even home lighting was by kerosene lamps with a thickly woven cloth wick. Sheep tallow candles were used as a substitute in emergencies. As late as 1860, commercial ice houses were still a rarity. Ice cream was made only during the winter months when snow was available to use in place of store-bought ice. And this was usually a family affair each Sunday after church.

In making soup, one popular old cook book advises: "First take great Care the Pots, or Sauce-pans and Covers be very clean, and free from all Grease and Sand, and that they are well tinned, for fear of giving the Broths and Soops a brassy Taste."

Baking delicious goodies such as Whipple's Johnny Cake Meal Pudding is much easier now than it was in early New England. Years ago when the housewife set out her Boston Cream Pie, her chewy ginger cookies, her browned currant loaf, she had a right to breathe a sigh of relief that the batch "turned out well." For there were times when the cookies were tough, the cakes flat and her bread coarse.

Abraham Whipple's Rhode Island Johnny Cake Meal Pudding
Rub butter the size of a hickory nut around the sides and bottom of a smooth iron kettle. When melted add some boiling water to stop the milk from burning. Now add one quart of milk. Let it boil up to top of kettle. Stir in fine Johnny-cake meal, sifting with left hand and holding the meal high so that every grain will be scalded, Stir constantly and add a little salt. Set away until cold, then add dark Molasses and cold milk and stir well. Pour into well buttered pudding dish. Cover and bake VERY SLOWLY for ten to twelve hours. Serve this hot and eat with plenty of fresh butter.

Abraham Whipple's Rhode Island Johnny Cake Meal Pudding

1 tablespoon butter
1/2 cup water, boiling
8 cups milk
2 cups cornmeal
1/4 teaspoon salt
2 cups dark molasses

Heat a large pot and grease it with the butter as it melts. Add the boiling water to the pot and then 4 cups of the milk. Bring this mixture to a boil and slowly stir in the corn meal and salt. Take the pot from the stove and continue to stir until thoroughly blended. Set aside to cool. When cold, stir in the molasses and the other 4 cups of milk. Pour into a well-greased baking pan and cover. Bake in a very slow oven (275 degrees) for 10 to 12 hours. Melt butter over each portion and serve while hot. In most modern adaptations of this old recipe, 1 teaspoon each of ginger, allspice and cinnamon are added to the mixture while it is still very hot. Then, after the mixture cools, 1 or 2 well beaten eggs are also stirred in thoroughly with the molasses and cold milk.

Abraham Whipple (1733-1819) was a famed naval officer who was born in Providence, Rhode Island. In 1759-60 he captained a privateer, capturing in a single cruise 26 French vessels. He was later a commodore and was put in command of two armed vessels fitted out by Rhode Island.

New England Clam Chowder—Noah Webster Style

1 cup salt pork,
    small cubes
2 onions, chopped fine
1 quart clams
4 large potatoes, diced
4 cups milk

1/2 cup butter
1 1/2 teaspoons salt
1 teaspoon pepper
1 garlic clove
2 cups cream
12 crackers

Fry the salt pork in a cast iron skillet until all the grease is extracted. Strain off the pieces of salt pork and add the onions. Gently sauté them until golden yellow. As Noah Webster once said: "Fried onions won't give people indigestion, unless they are fried brown or black." Put the clams in a saucepan with their own juice and heat until the edges curl. This will take only a couple of minutes. Set aside while parboiling the potatoes. "When the clams are cool enough to handle," advises Webster, "some people squeeze the dark part from their little bellies. This is done with the thumb and forefinger, and is not as surgical as it sounds. The necks are of no value except to the clam, and might as well be removed." Add the onions and potatoes to the clams in the saucepan. Stir in the milk and butter. Add the salt and pepper. Spear the garlic on a toothpick and let it float in the chowder. The toothpick will help locate the garlic when you want to remove it. "A proper chowder should marinate (simmer) on the back of the stove for an hour or more while the ingredients become thoroughly familiar with one another," explains Webster. After simmering for at least 1 hour, take out the garlic. Stir in the cream. Butter a dozen crackers and serve them on top of the chowder. Serve while hot.

Noah Webster was born in Hartford, Connecticut, October 16, 1758. His *American Spelling-book* was published in 1783. While in Philadelphia in 1787, he assisted in framing the Constitution.

NOAH WEBSTER.

William Evart's Boston Cream Pie

1 tablespoon butter   1/4 teaspoon salt
1/2 cup milk   2 eggs
1 cup flour   1 cup sugar
1 teaspoon baking powder   1 teaspoon vanilla

Add the butter to the milk in a saucepan and heat in a larger pot of hot water. Take a large wooden mixing bowl and sift together the flour, baking powder and salt. In another bowl, beat the eggs until they are thick. Then gradually beat in the sugar. Add the vanilla to this and gradually beat in the hot milk-butter mixture. Fold in the flour and blend thoroughly. Pour this batter into an 8 inch square baking pan greased with butter. Bake in a moderate oven (350 degrees) for 40 to 50 minutes. While this is baking, proceed to make the filling as follows:

2/3 cup sugar   2 cups milk, scalded
1/3 cup flour   1 egg, slightly beaten
1/8 teaspoon salt   1 teaspoon vanilla

Mix the sugar, flour and salt in a saucepan. Gradually pour on the scalded milk and set in a larger pan of hot water. Allow to cook until the mixture is smooth and thick (about 15 minutes). Stir constantly while cooking. Pour this over the beaten egg in a mixing bowl. Stir well and return to the saucepan. Cook for 2 more minutes, then stir in the vanilla. Split the warm cake and spread this cream filling between the layers. Sift 1/4 cup powdered sugar over the top. This cake is enough for 8 to 10 people.

William Evart also enjoyed this cake with raspberry jam spread between the layers. He was an attorney born in Boston in 1818. This man was the principal counsel for President Johnson at his impeachment trial. He also gained fame as counsel for Henry Ward Beecher in his defense against charges preferred by Theodore Tilton.

Nathanael Greene's Favorite Corned Beef and Cabbage

4 pounds corned beef
8 large carrots
1 large head cabbage, cut in 8 wedges
8 large potatoes, halved
2 tablespoons paprika
1 tablespoon salt
1/2 tablespoon pepper

Put the corned beef into a large cast iron kettle and cover with cold water. Bring to a boil and then allow to simmer for 4 hours. Pour some of the cooking liquid into another kettle. Add the carrots and potatoes and bring to a boil. Let this simmer for 15 minutes. Add the cabbage and let simmer another 15 minutes. Remove the corned beef from the first kettle. Sprinkle with paprika, salt and pepper. Place on a large platter and surround with cooked vegetables. Nathanael Greene warns that: "Corned beef is better if not reheated. Vegetables are best if cooked in corned beef liquid in a separate pot and not with the meat." This recipe will serve 8 people.

Greene was born in Rhode Island in 1742. He was a Quaker, but was disowned by them because of his military proclivities. He was a brigadier-general in Washington's Continental Army of 1775.

NATHANAEL GREENE.

Old Fashioned Oyster Ketchup of David Kinnison

DAVID KINNISON.

4 cups oysters
3/4 cup cider vinegar
3/4 cup sherry wine
1 teaspoon red pepper
1 tablespoon salt
6 teaspoons mace

Chop the oysters and boil them in their own liquor with the cider vinegar. Skim off the scum as it rises. Let this mixture boil a full 3 minutes, then strain through a piece of cheesecloth. Return the liquor to the kettle and immediately stir in the wine, salt, pepper and mace. Boil for another 15 minutes. Set aside to cool. When cold, pour into bottles and cork. Seal the corks by dipping them in melted wax.

David Kinnison was a New England patriot who was born on November 17, 1736, in Portsmouth, Maine. He was the last survivor of the "Boston Tea Party" when he died in 1851.

Chewy Ginger Cookies—A Favorite of Eli Whitney

1 cup butter
1 teaspoon salt
1 teaspoon baking soda
1 teaspoon cinnamon
1 teaspoon ginger

1 cup sugar
1 egg, well beaten
1 cup molasses
1/4 cup sour milk
4 cups flour, sifted

Take a wooden mixing bowl and put in the butter, salt, baking soda, cinnamon and ginger. Blend well. Then add the sugar and beat to a smooth cream. Put in the beaten egg and stir thoroughly. Add the molasses and sour milk. Gradually stir in the flour until the mixture is blended. Drop from the tip of a teaspoon on greased baking sheets. Let stand for 10 minutes, then flatten cookies by pressing with a glass covered with a damp cloth. Bake in a moderate oven (350 degrees) for 12 to 15 minutes. This recipe makes about 7 dozen old-fashioned ginger cookies.

Eli Whitney (1765-1825) dearly loved these cookies as made by his grandmother. He invented the cotton gin in 1792 when he was only 27 years old. This mechanical genius made nothing from his marvelous invention as everyone violated his patent without paying any royalties.

ELI WHITNEY.

Charles Sumner's Codfish Balls

CHARLES SUMNER.

2 cups raw potatoes, cut in small pieces
1 cup codfish, shredded
1/2 tablespoon butter
1/8 teaspoon pepper
1 egg, well beaten

Put the potatoes into a deep kettle and cover with cold water. Add the codfish and bring to a boil. Continue boiling until the potatoes are tender. Take the kettle from the stove and drain well. Stir in the butter and pepper. Beat the mixture with a fork. Then stir in the beaten egg and set aside to cool. Take a deep skillet and melt enough butter until it is 1 inch deep. Drop the fish mixture by tablespoons into the butter when hot and fry until golden brown. Drain on absorbent paper or cloth, garnish with parsley and serve immediately. This makes enough to serve 6 people.

Charles Sumner loved these golden-crisp fish balls. As a Senator in 1856, he delivered a speech vigorously attacking slaveholders. He was violently assaulted by Preston Brooks of South Carolina, and the injuries received compelled him to withdraw from his public duties for nearly 4 years.

Nathaniel Lyon's Famous Ginger Bread

1 cup molasses
1/2 cup butter
1/2 cup sugar
1 cup water, boiling
1 cup walnuts, chopped
1 cup raisins, chopped

3 cups flour
2 teaspoons baking powder
1/4 teaspoon salt
2 teaspoons cinnamon
1 teaspoon ginger
2 eggs, well beaten

Put the molasses into a wooden mixing bowl with the butter and sugar. Pour in the boiling water and stir well. Let this cool thoroughly, then add the walnuts and raisins. Sift together the flour, baking powder, salt, cinnamon and ginger. Add this to the mixture and stir until blended. Lastly, stir in the beaten eggs. Grease and flour a shallow baking pan. Put the gingerbread mixture in the baking pan and bake in a moderate oven (350 degrees) for 40 minutes. Let cool and cut in squares. Gingerbread is probably one of the oldest forms of cake known. It was formerly made of rye flour kneaded with ginger and other spices, and sweetened with honey.

Nathaniel Lyon (1818-1861) was a Connecticut Yankee killed in action during the Civil War. He never married and bequeathed his property to the government to assist in preserving the Union.

NATHANIEL LYON.

New England Boiled Dinner—Benjamin Wade Style

4 pounds smoked ham shank
8 large potatoes, pared and quartered
8 large turnips, pared and quartered
8 large carrots, pared and quartered
1 large head of cabbage, cut in wedges
3 teaspoons salt
2 teaspoons pepper

Put the ham shank into a large cast iron kettle and cover with cold water. Bring to a boil and cook until tender. Add the potatoes, turnips and carrots and let simmer for 40 minutes. Now add the cabbage and simmer for another 20 minutes. Season with the salt and pepper. This recipe serves 6 people. Benjamin Franklin Wade enjoyed this dish even more with beets, squash and quartered onions added. They should be put in with the cabbage.

Wade (1800-1878) was a conspicuous anti-slavery leader. He was acting Vice-President under Andrew Johnson.

Apple Fritter—Favorite of Rufus King

1 cup flour, sifted
1 1/4 teaspoons baking powder
1/4 teaspoon salt
1 egg, well beaten
1/2 cup milk
2 teaspoons butter, melted
2 large apples, pared and sliced
1 tablespoon lemon juice
1/4 teaspoon nutmeg
1/4 teaspoon cinnamon
2 tablespoons sugar

Sift the flour, baking powder and salt together in a large wooden mixing bowl. Combine the egg, milk and butter in another bowl, then add to the dry ingredients. Beat until smooth. Chill this batter to make the fritters lighter. Meanwhile, sprinkle apple slices with lemon juice, nutmeg, cinnamon and sugar. Dip apple slices in the chilled batter and deep fry in hot butter for 5 minutes, or until brown.

Rufus King (1755-1827) was born in Maine, and was a leading Federalist. He and General Schuyler were chosen the first representatives of New York in the national Senate of 1789, under the new Constitution. He said: "No end of fruit fritters may be made from this recipe. They're crisp, tender, digestible—and so good!"

Samuel Kirkland's Finest Currant Loaf

SAMUEL KIRKLAND.

WILLIAM LLOYD GARRISON.

1 egg
1/2 teaspoon salt
1 teaspoon cinnamon
2 tablespoons molasses
4 teaspoons baking powder
1/2 cup currants
1 cup milk
2 tablespoons butter, melted
2 cups flower

Beat the egg thoroughly in a wooden mixing bowl and then stir in the salt, cinnamon, molasses, currants, milk and melted butter. Then sift in the flour and baking powder. Blend well and pour into a well-greased baking pan. Bake in a moderate oven (350 degrees) for 45 minutes.

Samuel Kirkland (1741-1808) enjoyed this cake served warm with coffee or slices of the cake toasted with tea. He was a missionary who was born in Connecticut. He spent much of his time with Indians and was instrumental in securing the neutrality of the Six Nations.

William L. Garrison's Baked Beans

Garrison was born in Boston in 1804. He was an uncompromising opponent of slavery and founded the American Anti-Slavery Society in 1832. Here is his recipe for Boston Baked Beans in poetic form:

If, my dear housekeeper, you should ever wish,
  For breakfast or dinner a tempting dish,
Of the beans so famous in Boston town,
  You must read the rules I here lay down.
When the sun has set in golden light,
  And around you fall the shades of night,
A large, deep dish you first prepare;
  A quart of beans select with care;
And pick them over, until you find,
  Not a speck or a mote is left behind.
A lot of cold water on them pour,
  Till every bean is covered o'er,
And they seem to your poetic eye,
  Like pearls in the depth of the sea to lie;
Here, if you please, you may let them stay,
  Till just after breakfast the very next day,
When a parboiling process must be gone through,
  I mean for the beans, and not for you;

Then, if, in the pantry, there still should be,
  That bean pot, so famous in history.
With all due deference bring it out,
  And, if there's a skimmer lying about,
Skim half of the beans from the boiling pan,
  Into the bean pot as fast as you can;
Then turn to Biddy and calmly tell her,
  To take a huge knife and go to the cellar;
For you must have, like Shylock of old,
  'A pound of flesh,' ere your beans grow cold;
But, very unlike that ancient Jew,
  Nothing but pork will do for you.
Then tell once more your maiden fair,
  In the choice of the piece to take great care,
For a streak of fat or a streak of lean,
  Will give the right flavor to every bean!
This you must wash, and rinse, and score,
  Put into the pot, and 'round it pour,
The rest, till the view presented seems,
  Like an island of pork in an ocean of beans;
Pour on boiling hot water enough to cover,
  The tops of the beans completely over,
Shove into the oven and bake till done,
  And the triumph of Yankee cookery's won!

The Colonial kitchen in the Wanton-Lyman-Hazard home in early
Rhode Island. *Courtesy of the Preservation Society of Newport
County, Newport, Rhode Island.*

A Taste of the Old West

In depicting early ranch and range life, movie-makers and story-tellers usually mention, then dismiss, one of the most colorful and important characters of the west. In fact, this often ignored but imminently worthy fellow wielded more influence than the ranch foreman, the trail boss and sometimes more than the owner of the spread, himself! He was the cook.

Back at the ranch, he presided over the cookshack in kingly solitude, secure that if he was good at what he did, his reign was virtually unassailable. The reason for his lofty position is obvious. Next to sleep, he provided the one thing cowhands cherished most. Well-fed cowpunchers were happy cowpunchers, and happy cowpunchers stayed put.

Mrs. Burt's Fort Laramie Chicken Salad
Mix 1 heaping teaspoon fine mustard, the yolk of a fresh egg and a teaspoon of fresh wine or cider vinegar into a smooth paste using a silver fork. Measure out 6 tablespoons pure salad oil and 1 tablespoon each of vinegar and lemon juice. Mix slowly, making a creamy paste. Take a cold boiled chicken, remove the skin, bones and fat, and chop—not too fine. Cut up an equal bulk of celery, mix with the chicken. Add a saltspoon salt and half of the dressing. Cover the bottom of the platter with the larger leaves of lettuce, and lay the smaller green leaves around the border. Place the salad in the dish and pour the remainder of the dressing over it. Garnish with parsley, capers, olives and hard-boiled eggs. If celery cannot be found, use white tender cabbage mixed with a teaspoon of extract of celery. If salad dressing curdles, stir in half a teaspoon vinegar or lemon alone. Mix well, and if that doesn't bring it right, set it in the ice box for a while. If it still curdles, take another yolk and gradually stir into the curdled sauce, and it will come all right.

Mrs. Burt's Fort Laramie Chicken Salad

4 cups celery, chopped
1/2 teaspoon salt
Lettuce—small head
1 teaspoon parsley
1 teaspoon capers
12 olives, quartered
6 eggs, hardboiled, sliced

Blend the mustard, raw egg yolk, and the wine or cider vinegar until you have a thick, smooth paste. Then stir in the olive oil, vinegar and lemon juice. Set this concoction aside as you thoroughly blend the chicken (when cold), celery and salt in a separate wooden bowl. Now mix half the previously made dressing in with this. Dump the salad onto a platter lined with lettuce leaves. Pour the remainder of the dressing over this. Lastly, garnish with the parsley, capers, olives and hardboiled eggs.

Elizabeth Burt was the wife of the commander of Fort Laramie, Wyoming. She wrote her *Cookbook* in 1870.

1 teaspoon mustard
1 egg yolk
1 teaspoon wine vinegar or
1 teaspoon cider vinegar
6 tablespoons olive oil
1 tablespoon vinegar
1 tablespoon lemon juice
1 boiled chicken, chopped

Sam Houston's Famed Texas Barbecue Sauce

3 tablespoons cooking oil
1/4 cup onion, grated
1 garlic clove, crushed
1 cup catsup
1/4 cup Worcestershire sauce
1/4 cup lemon juice
2 tablespoons white vinegar
1 teaspoon hot pepper sauce
3/4 teaspoon salt
2 tablespoons sugar
2 teaspoons paprika
1 1/2 teaspoons chili powder
1 tablespoon dry mustard
2 teaspoons water

Heat the cooking oil in a large heavy cast iron skillet. Add the onion and the garlic. Sauté this lightly. Stir in the catsup, Worcestershire sauce, lemon juice, white vinegar, hot pepper sauce, sugar, paprika, chili powder and salt. Blend together thoroughly the dry mustard and the water until smooth. Then stir this into the sauce. Slowly bring this mixture to a boil. Cover and let simmer for 20 minutes. It makes 2 cups. Sam Houston used this spicy concoction both as a marinade and a basting sauce for his barbecued steaks, chops and chicken.

Custer's Favorite Dakota Fried Tomatoes

Slice the green tomatoes. Salt and pepper each slice liberally. Then dip these slices in flour until each is thickly covered. Deep fry in hot oil until nicely browned. Drain the fried slices on brown paper. When all the slices are fried and draining, empty the skillet of excess cooking oil. Now put in the cream or milk. Add 1 tablespoon flour to thicken. Stir in the butter, salt and pepper. Blend well. Place the fried tomatoes in a bowl and pour this mixture over them. Serve immediately. Green tomatoes cooked in this manner are delightfully delicious with or without the pan gravy as above. Ripe tomatoes can also be fried for a totally different taste variation.

General George Armstrong Custer (1839-76) enjoyed this particular dish often during his lifetime. His mother usually made it with green tomatoes, since these were George's favorite. Custer gained fame as an Indian fighter against the Cheyennes from 1867 to 1868. His military force was obliterated by Sitting Bull's warriors at Little Big Horn.

6 large green tomatoes
Shaker of salt
Shaker of pepper
3 cups flour
1 cup cream or
1 cup milk

1 tablespoon flour
1 tablespoon butter,
  melted
1/2 teaspoon salt
1/4 teaspoon pepper

Beef Steak and Oysters California

1 pound steak
1/2 cup small oysters, fresh
2 tablespoons butter
1 1/2 tablespoons flour
1/4 cup water
1/2 lime, juice only
1/4 teaspoon salt

1/4 teaspoon pepper
1 clove garlic,
    chopped fine
1 tablespoon pimento,
    chopped
1/2 teaspoon parsley,
    chopped

Put the steak on to broil. Meanwhile, place the oysters and their juice in a saucepan with the butter. Simmer until the edges of the oysters curl. Then take out the oysters and chop them up fine. Set aside until later. Now slowly stir in the flour and mix well until no lumps are evident. Add the water to thin the gravy. Then stir in the lime juice, salt, pepper and garlic. Lastly, blend in the chopped oysters. When the steak is done the way you want it, pour this delightful mixture over it. Garnish with the pimento and the parsley. This delicious old recipe was long ago a specialty of the famous Palace Hotel in San Francisco. General Grant (1822-85) enjoyed steak prepared in this manner while staying at the Palace.

Mrs. Bonney's Montana Blind Rabbit

1 cup bread crumbs, soaked well
1 egg, well beaten
1/2 pound pork, ground
1/2 pound beef, ground
1/2 pound veal, ground
1 teaspoon salt
1/2 teaspoon pepper
1/2 lemon, juice only

Blend all of the above ingredients in a large wooden mixing bowl. Then pack in a loaf pan and bake in a moderate oven (350 degrees) for 1 hour.

Mrs. Bonney often fixed this treat for her son, William Henry Bonney, later to be known as the notorious Billy the Kid. They lived in Silver City, Montana, at the time.

Belle Starr's Oklahoma Territory Beef Soup

1 medium bay leaf
1/4 teaspoon thyme
3 quarts water
1 tablespoon salt
1 teaspoon pepper
1 cup flour
2 tablespoons catsup
1/2 glass sherry wine

2 pounds beef, cut up into 1 inch cubes
2 tablespoons butter
2 carrots, sliced
3 onions, sliced
2 turnips, sliced
1 leek, cut up
1 bunch celery, cut up
2 tablespoons parsley, chopped
2 thick slices salt pork, diced

Put the cut up beef chunks into a large stew pan with the salt pork and the butter. Add all of the vegetables and herbs. Put in 1 cup of the water and bring to a boil. Stir over the heat until the meat juices are drawn. Then pour in the rest of the water, and when this comes to a boil, add the salt and pepper. Then carefully skim and let it all simmer together for 4 hours, or until the meat pieces are tender. Take out the meat, again skim, and then strain the soup. Thicken the liquor with flour and flavor with the catsup and the wine. Lastly, put the meat back in, simmer for 5 minutes and serve. This famed old recipe was a favorite of Belle Starr (1848-89), the Bandit Queen of the wild West.

General Winfield Scott's Mexican Corn Bread Deluxe

1 1/4 cups yellow cornmeal
1/2 teaspoon baking soda
3/4 teaspoon salt
3 cups creamed corn
2 eggs, well beaten
1/4 cup butter, melted
1 cup milk
3 cups cheese, grated
1 onion, grated
2 red peppers, chopped fine

General Scott became acquainted with this delicious cornmeal dish while in New Mexico during the Mexican War in 1847. He won the now forgotten battles of Cérro Gordo, Contreras and Churubusco. This man was nominated as Whig candidate for the Presidency, but was unsuccessful.

Blend the cornmeal, baking soda and salt in a large wooden mixing bowl. Then stir in the creamed corn, the frothy beaten eggs, melted butter, milk and 1 cup of the cheese. When thoroughly blended, pour 1/2 the batter into a well-greased 10-inch square baking pan. Now mix the rest of the cheese, the onion and the red peppers together. Sprinkle this over the batter in the pan. Pour the remaining batter over this. Bake in a moderate oven (350 degrees) for 45 minutes, or until done. Serve while hot.

Brigham Young's Skillet Cookies

3 1/2 cups flour
1 cup sugar
1 1/2 teaspoons baking powder
1/2 teaspoon baking soda
1 teaspoon salt
1 teaspoon nutmeg
1 cup shortening
1 egg, beaten
1/2 cup milk
1 1/4 cup raisins

Mix the first 6 dry ingredients. Then chop the shortening into these dry ingredients with a fork until crumbly. Beat the egg until frothy. Add the milk to the beaten egg and stir. Now add the egg-milk mixture to the dry ingredients and blend. Lastly, stir in the raisins. Roll out the dough on a lightly floured surface to 1/4 inch thickness. Cut with a floured cookie cutter. Place these treats on a heated, greased cast iron skillet and cook until lightly browned on one side. Turn and brown the other side. This makes about 4 dozen marvelous cookies. Brigham also liked another variation of these cookies. He sometimes had his wives substitute 1 tablespoon grated lemon rind in place of the raisins.

Kearney's Famous Kansas Chicken Scrapple

4 cups chicken broth
1 1/3 cups cornmeal
1 tablespoon flour
1 1/4 teaspoons salt
1/4 teaspoon poultry seasoning
2 1/2 cups cooked chicken, finely ground

Heat 2 cups of the chicken broth in a large pan. In a wooden mixing bowl, blend the cornmeal, flour, salt and poultry seasoning. Mix these dry ingredients with the unheated broth. Slowly stir this mixture into the hot broth. Cook and continuously stir over a low heat until the mixture thickens. Cover the pan and let it cook slowly for 15 minutes longer, stirring as required to keep it from sticking. Now add the ground chicken and stir for 2 minutes longer. Pour into a well-greased loaf pan and chill until firm. Remove from the pan and cut into 1/4 inch thick slices. Roll each slice in flour and put in a heated, greased frying pan. Brown on both sides and serve while hot. This recipe makes 6 servings.

General Kearney left Fort Leavenworth, Kansas, in June of 1846, to forcibly take the Mexican provinces of California and New Mexico. The women at the fort also made a delightful pork scrapple by substituting pork for the chicken and water or meat stock in place of the chicken broth.

Buffalo Bill Cody's Favorite Cabbage Dish

1 large head cabbage, boiled
1 tablespoon butter, melted
1 teaspoon salt
1/4 teaspoon pepper
4 tablespoons cream
2 eggs, well beaten

Finely chop up the cold head of boiled cabbage. Let it drain until very dry. Then stir in the melted butter, salt, pepper, cream and frothy beaten eggs. Put this mixture into a buttered cast iron skillet and slowly heat. Stir until it becomes smoking hot. Then let it stand just long enough for the cabbage to brown slightly on the underside. Lay a flat dish over the pan, upside down, and turn the fried cabbage out of the skillet. Serve while hot.

This early American breakfast dish was served to William Frederick Cody (1846-1917) long before he ever became so widely known as "Buffalo Bill." It was an old Cody family recipe that was handed down for a great number of years.

Kit Carson's Pack Mule Indian Pudding

2 cups cornmeal
4 cups milk, boiling
1 cup molasses
1 tablespoon butter
3 eggs, well beaten

1 lemon, peel only, grated
    or
1 cup raisins
1 teaspoon cinnamon
1/2 teaspoon ginger

Put the cornmeal into a large bowl and pour the boiling milk over it. Stir until thoroughly mixed and set aside to cool. Meanwhile, blend the molasses and the butter in a saucepan. Heat slowly and stir until the butter all melts. Then stir in the beaten eggs, grated lemon peel or raisins (or both if desired), cinnamon and ginger. Pour this mixture into the cornmeal and milk in the wooden bowl and blend well. Lastly, put it all in a greased baking pan and bake in a slow oven (300 degrees) for 1 hour. This marvelous pudding is to be eaten with a sauce made of beaten butter and sugar. It was a favorite of the great mountain man, Kit Carson, who guided John Fremont on his historic Western trek.

Prospector's Brown Beans and Dumplings

1 1/2 cups pinto beans
3 quarts water
1 small ham bone
1 large sweet potato, chopped
1 small onion, chopped
1 teaspoon salt

Put the beans and the water in a large pot. Bring to a boil and let this boil for 12 minutes. Take from the stove, cover, and let stand for 1 hour. Then add the ham bone, again cover the pot, and cook the beans until they are soft (about 2 hours). Now stir in the sweet potato, onion and salt. Cook for 30 more minutes.

While the beans are cooking, start making the dumplings. The ingredients required are:

1 cup sifted flour
1 1/2 teaspoons baking powder
1/2 teaspoon salt
1 tablespoon shortening
1 egg, beaten
1/4 cup milk

First sift the flour with the baking powder and the salt. Cut in the shortening with a fork until the mixture is as fine as cornmeal. Add the beaten egg and the milk. Stir lightly until a soft dough is formed. Drop pieces of the dough from a teaspoon onto the cooking bean mixture. Cover and cook for 12 minutes longer. The pot must be kept covered while cooking the dumplings to prevent sogginess.

This was a favorite of Captain Camillus Carr of Camp McDowell in 1866 Arizona. The recipe was given to his wife by an old prospector who was traveling through the area.

Indian Style Food Preparation

One of the chief contributions of the Indians to New England pioneers was the clambake. No one can dispute the old Indian method of "making a bake." Each bake had its own bakemaster who served year after year, sometimes for a lifetime. He supervised all the preparations from the building of the fire to the careful placing of the clams and the rest of the bake.

A delicacy of the western Indian was broiled buffalo marrow bones. They split the thigh bones and browned the marrow. This was then spread on cakes, breads and bean balls. Later, the white man called this popular dish "Prairie Butter."

The "iron ration" of the Sioux warriors was pemican. They roasted jerky until crisp, pounded it into meal, then added fat and berries. Balls were made, fried, and coated with suet grease to make them last while on the long hunt. And according to Lewis and Clark, the Sioux used a lot of sunflower seed meal in their varied dishes.

The Indians had no iron pots or kettles. They often cooked in a beef or buffalo paunch which was hung between four wooden posts. Of course, the "pot" was also eaten when the meal was done.

Koo Wes Koo We's Bread and Butter Molasses Pudding
Slice and break up some bread, spread well with butter and lay in a baking dish with currants between each layer of bread. Pour over this an unboiled custard made by beating eggs, milk, sugar and salt and some molasses. Let stand for two hours. Bake one hour. A rim of pastry around the edge makes all puddings look better, but is not necessary.

Koo Wes Koo Kee's Bread and Butter Molasses Pudding

8 slices stale bread, cubed
1 cup seedless raisins
2 eggs
1/2 teaspoon salt
3 tablespoons molasses
3 teaspoons sugar
2 tablespoons butter
2 1/2 cups milk, scalded

Cover the bottom of a well-buttered baking pan with all of the stale bread crumbs. Then stir in the raisins. Beat the eggs, salt, molasses and sugar together. Melt the butter in the scalded milk. Stir this into the egg mixture and blend thoroughly. Pour over the stale bread cubes. Place the baking pan in another pan of hot water and bake in a moderate oven (350 degrees) for 1 hour, or until the pudding is firm to the touch. This pudding should be served with whipped cream. It will feed 6 people.

Koo Wes Koo We was the Indian name of John Ross, a Cherokee chief, born in Georgia in 1790. He became principal chief of the Cherokee nation in 1828, and from the very beginning was an efficient champion of their rights against the encroachments and cupidity of the white man. When the Civil War broke out the Cherokees joined the Confederacy, over the protests of Ross.

Sagoyewatha's Pumpkin Soup

6 cups pumpkin, stewed	3/4 teaspoon marjoram
6 cups cream	1/2 teaspoon cinnamon
or	1/2 teaspoon mace
6 cups milk	1 1/2 teaspoon salt
3 tablespoons brown sugar	1/4 teaspoon pepper
3 tablespoons molasses	1 1/2 teaspoon orange
	extract

Put the pumpkin and the cream or milk into a small cast iron kettle and blend well. Simmer over a low heat for 5 minutes while stirring constantly. Stir in the brown sugar, molasses, marjoram, cinnamon, mace, salt, pepper and orange extract. Continue stirring until the mixture comes to a boil. This soup is delicious either hot or cold.

Sagoyewatha (Red Jacket) was chief of the Seneca Wolf tribe. Born in 1751, he served the British King during the Revolutionary War. His people later became the allies of the Americans against the British in the War of 1812. He derived his name, "Red Jacket," from wearing a British coat into battle. He was known as the most inveterate enemy of the missionaries sent to his nation, and he never yielded to the influences of Christianity.

Elkswatawa's Best Squaw Cake

ELKSWATAWA, THE PROPHET.

2 cups sugar
3/4 cup bacon grease
2 cups water
    or
2 cups milk
1 cup raisins
1 teaspoon cloves

1 teaspoon nutmeg
1 teaspoon allspice
1/2 teaspoon salt
3 1/2 cups flour
1 teaspoon baking soda
2 teaspoons baking powder
1 cup nuts, chopped

Put the sugar and bacon grease into a cast iron pot and heat. Stir in the water or milk, raisins, cloves, nutmeg, allspice and salt. Bring to a boil and allow to boil for 5 minutes, stirring occasionally. Take the pot from the stove and allow to cool. Sift together the flour, baking soda and baking powder. Add this to the cooled mixture and beat thoroughly. Stir in the nuts. Pour batter into a buttered baking pan and bake in a moderate oven (350 degrees) for 40 minutes. This squaw cake is to be eaten plain or sprinkled with some powdered sugar.

Elkswatawa was known as the Prophet. He was the brother of the famous Tecumseh, born 1775 in Piqua, the seat of the Piqua clan of the Shawnees. This Indian gained fame as a "medicine man" among his people and was believed to possess great powers of divination.

Leather Britches—A Favorite of Sitting Bull

2 pounds green beans
4 quarts water
1/2 pound salt pork, ground
4 teaspoons salt
1/4 teaspoon pepper

Break the ends off the green beans and puncture the end of each bean. Run a string through each bean and hang in the sun for at least 2 months. Before cooking, put the beans in a large cast iron kettle with 4 quarts cold water. Allow to soak for 2 hours. Stir in the salt pork, salt and pepper. Bring to a quick boil. Then let simmer for 3 hours. Stir occasionally while they simmer. More water may be added if necessary, because these beans are to be eaten with plenty of hot broth. Serve with corn bread or corn pone.

Sitting Bull was the Sioux chief of the Dakota and Wyoming Territory in the 1860s. He was an outstanding warrior and shrewd politician. He once said: "We are an island of Indians in a lake of whites." In 1876, Sitting Bull faced U.S. Army troops led by George Custer. He and 4,000 warriors destroyed the cavalrymen in the Big Horn Mountains.

SITTING BULL.

Indian Clam Bake from Early Times

The original Indian clambake hasn't really changed over the years. It is made with soft-shell clams preferably about 2 inches long. A fire of cordwood is built on a layer of stones, each about the size of a man's hand. The fire is allowed to burn until the stones become white hot. A proper fire will heat the stones in approximately 1 hour. Then the wood embers are removed with 6-tined potato diggers and pitchforks. The stones are swept clean of ashes. A thick layer of rockweed, a marine growth commonly found along the shores, is thrown on the hot stones.

First the fresh clams are placed on the steaming rockweed, and covered with another layer. Then add the following: white and sweet potatoes still in their skins; sweet corn on the cob covered with a thin layer of husks; fish in cloth or paper bags (bluefish is preferred although mackerel will do); small sausages or buckworsts similarly wrapped; and lobsters.

Then cover all this with a thick wet piece of canvas and keep it wet all during the baking. The steam from the salty moisture of the clams and rockweed permeates, tenderizes, and flavors everything. This steam is carefully confined by covering the edges of the canvas with rockweed and holding it down with stones. Even then, the mouth-watering fragrance of the bake escapes during the 45 minutes it takes to cook. There are traditional accompanying foods always found on the serving tables. These include sliced cucumbers, sliced tomatoes and sliced raw onions. Other necessities are brown bread, white bread and butter, pepper, salt, vinegar, pepper sauce, and small pitchers of melted butter.

The initial course of a clambake is always a bowl of clam chowder served with clam fritters. When the bake is opened, dishes holding 2 quarts of clams are served to each guest. The clam shells are easily spread apart with the fingers. Remove the covering of the clam snout. Take the clam by the snout and dip it in a small dish of hot melted butter. This is usually blended with a little vinegar or perhaps a dash of pepper sauce. You then eat the clams with the exception of the snout, which is tough. The clambake traditionally ends by drinking fresh coffee.

Geronimo's Apache Stew

3 pounds round steak
1 cup acorns, ground fine
1 teaspoon salt
1/2 teaspoon pepper

Cut the steak into 1 inch squares and put in a large cast iron kettle with 6 cups water. Bring to a boil and then allow to simmer for 4 hours. Strain the broth from the meat and set aside to use later. Shred the pieces of beef and blend with the acorn flour. Pour the hot broth over this, add the salt and pepper and stir until well blended. Let simmer for 10 minutes and it is ready to serve.

Geronimo loved fried bread with this stew. He was the leader of the Chiricahuas in 1876, an autonomous Apache band in the Arizona and New Mexico Territories. He took over as warlord when Cochise died. Geronimo was the bitterest and bloodiest fighter the white man had ever battled in the West. He died in 1907.

GERONIMO.

Chief Hendrick's Plum-Peach Jam

HENDRICK.

10 cups plums, fresh, cut in small pieces
16 cups sugar (8 pounds)
8 cups peaches, fresh, cut in small pieces
2 lemons, thinly sliced

Put all of the ingredients in a large cast iron kettle and stir well. Bring to a boil and stir constantly until the mixture becomes quite thick. Remove from the stove and skim, then stir, alternately for 7 minutes. Pour the mixture into heated pint jars and seal. Set aside to cool and use when needed. This recipe makes 12 pints of marvelous jam.

Hendrick was a Mohawk chief who was born in 1680. In 1755 he joined General William Johnson with 200 Mohawk warriors at the head of Lake George. He and his followers were ambushed at Rocky Brook and he was slain, September 8, 1755.

Randolph's Yam Loaf

2 tablespoons butter
1 small onion, chopped
1 tablespoon flour
1/2 teaspoon salt
1/8 teaspoon pepper

1 cup milk
1 cup bread crumbs, soft
1 cup nuts, chopped fine
2 cups sweet potatoes,
    mashed

Melt the butter in a cast iron skillet and brown the onion in this. Stir in the flour, salt and pepper. Add the milk and simmer until the mixture becomes thick. Add the bread crumbs, nuts and sweet potatoes. Blend thoroughly and place the skillet in a moderate oven (350 degrees) for 30 minutes or until nicely browned. Or you may make delicious Indian yam cakes by placing small balls of this mixture on a baking sheet and baking in a hot oven (425 degrees) for 10 to 20 minutes. Serve while hot, or split them when cold and toast.

John Randolph (1773-1833) was a descendant of Pocahontas, and a great-grandson of William Randolph, the colonist. He fought a duel with Henry Clay in 1826. Randolph frequently indulged in grossly insulting his opponents while a Senator from 1825 to 1827. He advocated State supremacy and often stood alone.

Indian Apple Baked Dish

1/2 cup corn meal
3 cups milk, scalded
1 teaspoon cinnamon
1 teaspoon salt
1 1/2 cups brown sugar
2 cups milk, cold
2 tablespoons butter, melted
4 cups apples, cut in eights

Sift the corn meal into the scalded milk, stirring rapidly, and allow to simmer for 5 minutes. Remove from the stove and stir in the cinnamon, salt, brown sugar, cold milk, melted butter and apple pieces. When well blended, pour into a buttered baking pan and cover. Bake in a slow oven (300 degrees) for 4 hours. This old Indian recipe feeds 8 people.

Navaho Bean Balls

4 cups pinto beans
8 cups corn meal
1 cup flour
2 teaspoons baking soda

Put the beans in a large cast iron kettle and cover with cold water. Bring to a boil and then simmer until the beans are soft. Now put the corn meal in a large wooden mixing bowl and stir in the flour and baking soda. Blend well and add the hot beans to this mixture. Add enough water from the kettle to make a stiff dough. Roll this dough into small balls. Bring the bean liquid in the kettle to a boil and drop in the bean balls. Let simmer for 30 minutes and serve while hot.

Chief Osceola's Fried Squash Blossoms

3 dozen squash blossoms, freshly picked
1 cup cream
1 tablespoon flour
1 teaspoon salt
1/8 teaspoon pepper
1/2 cup butter

Put the fresh squash blossoms (If you grow your own squash, you can pick your own squash blossoms. If not, they are generally available at health food stores.) in a large wooden mixing bowl. Combine the cream, flour, salt and pepper in a pint jar, cover, and shake until perfectly blended. Pour this mixture over the squash blossoms in the mixing bowl. Melt the butter in a cast iron skillet. Heat the skillet and drop a little water on it. If the water sizzles, the skillet is ready. Put in the squash blossoms, one at a time, so they won't stick together. Fry until nicely browned. Take from the skillet and drain on absorbent paper or cloth. Sprinkle each blossom with a little paprika and serve while very hot. This recipe makes enough to serve 8 people.

Osceola (Black Drink) was a Seminole Indian chief born in 1804. From the beginning Osceola opposed the removal of the Seminoles from Florida. He led them in a war which began in 1835 and continued for about 7 years. He was actually a half-breed, the son of Willis Powell, an Englishman and trader, and a Creek Indian woman.

Chief Joseph's Homemade Bread

CHIEF JOSEPH.

1 tablespoon flour	2 teaspoons sugar
1 cup corn meal	1 cup milk, cold
2 teaspoons baking powder	1 egg
1/8 teaspoon salt	1/4 cup butter, melted

Put the flour and the corn meal in a large wooden mixing bowl and blend well. Stir in the baking powder, salt and sugar. Beat in the cold milk and the egg. Continue beating for 1 full minute. Put the melted butter in a 9 inch by 5 inch bread pan and run it up the sides. Pour your batter into this butter and bake in a hot oven (425 degress) for 25 to 30 minutes.

Chief Joseph especially liked this bread because of the hard crust it had. He was head of the Nez Percés and always tried his best to avoid conflicts with the white man. Finally, with his back to the wall after innumerable injustices, and a ruthless army attack on his people, he fought until his tribe was very nearly wiped out. Joseph was a native of the Idaho Territory, a pacifist who was reared by missionaries.

Traditional Old Southern Flavor

First and foremost, of course, the Southern housewife cooked. But a cook also did some doctoring, some barbering, a lot of sewing, and plenty of arbitrating with the business end of a cast iron skillet. Hot corn breads are a symbol of the early homemaker's southern hospitality. She never served cold bread! It was to be taken as a sign that the guest was unwelcome!

In the early south, Wise's Creole Corn Muffins, Beauregard's Pound Cake, and Hood's Scalloped Oysters were all baked in a wood heated oven. Baking was a matter of "guess." The woman of the house relied on when the oven "felt" hot enough to bake in. As one early observer states: "The cook would stick her bare arm in the oven and count 1001, 1002, etc., and if her arm was well burned the oven was ready for the bread."

Lye-treated corn was popularly eaten as a main dish in the old days of the south. It was called hominy. All coffee beans, until after the Civil War, were purchased green. The housewife had to both roast and grind her own coffee.

John Bell Hood's Scalloped Oysters
Having opened your oysters into a basin, and washed them out of their own liquor, put some into your scallop-shells, and strew over them a few crumbs of bread. Lay a slice of butter on them, then more oysters, bread and butter, successively, till your shell be as full as you intend it. Put them into a Dutch-oven to brown, and serve them up in shells in which they are scalloped.

John Bell Hood's Scalloped Oysters

2 tablespoons oyster liquor
2 tablespoons cream or
2 tablespoons milk

Blend the bread crumbs and cracker crumbs in a wooden mixing bowl. Stir in the melted butter. Put a thin layer of this mixture on the bottom of a well-buttered, shallow baking pan. Cover with oysters and sprinkle with salt and pepper. Add 1 tablespoon of the oyster liquor and 1 tablespoon of the cream. Repeat this entire process once again. Cover the top with the remaining crumbs. Bake in a hot oven (425 degrees) for 30 minutes. Never allow more than 2 layers for scalloped oysters. If 3 or more layers are used, the middle layers will not be properly cooked.

According to Mrs. Hood, "This is a very nice preparation of oysters." It was her son's, General John Bell Hood (1831-79), best-liked dish. He was the Confederate general who was soundly defeated by Sherman during the siege of Atlanta from July 22 to September 2, 1864. His continued failures during the Civil War led to his being relieved of command in 1865.

1/2 cup bread crumbs
1 cup cracker crumbs
1/2 cup butter, melted
2 cups oysters
2 teaspoons salt
1 teaspoon pepper

Southern Fried Chicken—Daniel Boone Style

*3 pound frying chicken,
    cut in serving pieces*
1/2 cup butter
1/4 cup water
1 1/2 tablespoons flour

1/2 teaspoon salt
1/8 teaspoon pepper
1/2 teaspoon paprika
1 cup water, boiling
2 tablespoons cream

Roll the pieces of chicken in a wooden mixing bowl of flour heavily seasoned with salt, pepper and paprika. Grease a large cast iron skillet with the butter and fry each piece of chicken. Brown well on both sides. Then reduce the heat slightly and add the water. Cover the skillet and cook for 15 minutes on each side. Take the fried chicken from the skillet and pour off all but 2 tablespoons butter. Add the flour to the melted butter, blend well, and stir until nicely browned. Then add the salt, pepper, paprika and boiling water. Simmer until the gravy is smooth and thickened, stirring constantly. Lastly, stir in the cream and blend. Pour this gravy around the chicken on a large platter.

As Daniel Boone says: "There's no better way to cook young chicken." This old fried chicken recipe originated in the family of Daniel Boone (1735-1820), the pioneer who is noted for his many daring exploits against the Indians. Boone's remains are interred near Frankfort, Kentucky.

Henry Wise's Creole Corn Muffins

HENRY ALEXANDER WISE.

1 1/2 cups flour
3 teaspoons baking powder
1 teaspoon salt
3 tablespoons sugar
3/4 cup corn meal
1 egg, well beaten
1/4 cup butter, melted
1 cup milk

1 tablespoon green pepper, chopped fine
1 teaspoon onion, chopped fine
1 cup cheese, grated

Take a large wooden mixing bowl and sift together the flour, baking powder, salt and sugar. Stir in the corn meal and blend well. Combine the beaten egg, melted butter and milk in another bowl. Pour this into the dry ingredients and stir vigorously until all the flour is dampened. Blend in the green pepper, onion and cheese. Pour batter into well greased muffin tins. Bake in a rather quick oven (400 degrees) for 25 to 30 minutes. The recipe makes 12 lovely muffins. This same batter can be used to make crispy creole puffs. Simply drop the batter from a wooden spoon into a kettle of hot deep grease and fry until golden brown.

Henry Alexander Wise (1806-1876) was governor of Virginia from 1856 to 1860. The last important act of his administration was ordering the execution of John Brown for the raid on Harper's Ferry. He was a zealous advocate of the annexation of Texas and believed it was the right of Congress to protect slavery. He was later a Confederate general.

Stuffed Eggplant—A Favorite of Jefferson Davis

2 large eggplants
2 tablespoons onion,
  minced
1 cup celery, chopped
1/2 teaspoon pepper
1 teaspoon salt

1/2 teaspoon nutmeg
1 teaspoon parsley
1 cup nuts, chopped
1/2 cup butter, melted
2 cups tomatoes,
  stewed
1/2 cup cream

3 tablespoons cream
1 tablespoon flour
1 teaspoon parsley

Put the eggplants in a cast iron kettle and cover with cold water. Parboil them for 10 minutes. Take the eggplants from the kettle and slit each down the side. Take out the seeds and lay the eggplants in a bowl of cold, salted water while preparing the stuffing as follows: Grease a cast iron skillet with butter and fry the onion and celery until nicely browned. Blend these with the rest of the ingredients in a wooden mixing bowl. Fill the cavity of each eggplant with this stuffing. Wind thread around them to keep the slit shut. Place the eggplants on the rack of a roasting pan. Put a little water in the bottom of the pan and bake in a moderate oven (350 degrees) for 25 minutes. Baste with melted butter and water as they bake. Now make the gravy:

Add the cream to the drippings in the bottom of the roasting pan. Thicken this with the flour and then stir in the parsley. Bring to a quick boil and pour over the eggplant on a large platter. Serve immediately. Varna Davis often prepared this delightful dish for her husband while he was President of the Confederacy in 1861.

JEFFERSON DAVIS.

Creamy Rice Pudding Special of Alexander Stephens

4 cups milk
1/4 teaspoon salt
1/2 cup rice, long grained
1/2 cup raisins
1 teaspoon nutmeg
1 cup cream
2 eggs, well beaten
1/2 cup sugar
1 teaspoon vanilla

Put the milk and salt into a saucepan and when warmed, add the rice. Bring to a quick boil and then allow to simmer for 15 minutes. Stir occasionally. Add the raisins and let it all simmer for 5 minutes longer. Stir in 1/4 cup of the cream and simmer for 3 more minutes, stirring constantly. Combine the frothy beaten eggs in a wooden mixing bowl with the sugar, vanilla and the rest of the cream. Blend well and stir in a tablespoon of the hot rice mixture from the saucepan. Then dump the contents of the mixing bowl into the saucepan and simmer slowly until it begins to thicken. At this point, pour the pudding into a clean bowl and stir often until it cools completely. Serve cold with nutmeg sprinkled over the top.

Alexander H. Stephens is an often forgotten man in the history of our great nation. He was vice-president of the Confederacy under Jefferson Davis in 1861.

Robertson's Special Old-Time Crullers

2 eggs
6 egg yolks
3/4 cup sugar
2 tablespoons cream
2 tablespoons butter,
  melted

2 tablespoons brandy
3 cups flour
2 teaspoons baking
  powder
1 teaspoon mace
1/4 teaspoon salt

Put the whole eggs and egg yolks in a wooden mixing bowl and beat until they are light. Add the sugar and beat another 10 minutes. Then stir in the cream, melted butter and brandy. Sift in together the flour, baking powder, mace and salt. Blend well. Drop a large spoon of dough at a time onto a well floured surface and knead lightly until the dough is stiff enough to roll out. Roll out thin and cut into oblong pieces about 3 1/2 inches long and 1 1/2 inches wide. Cut a 1 inch slit in the center of each, and pull one end through this opening. Fry to a golden brown in smoking hot grease, turning once. Drain on absorbent paper or a cloth and dust with powdered sugar before serving. This old recipe makes 35 crullers. Mrs. Robertson explains: "Cruller dough should be as soft as can be handled and little or no additional flour worked in when kneading, as this will make them solid and dry."

James Robertson is best known as "the father of Tennessee."

JAMES ROBERTSON

Robert E. Lee's Fish Timbales

ROBERT E. LEE.

1/2 cup cream
2 tablespoons stale bread crumbs
1 teaspoon parsley
1 cup salmon, cooked
3 egg yolks, well beaten
1 tablespoon lemon juice
1/4 teaspoon onion juice
1/4 teaspoon salt
1/4 teaspoon pepper

Put the cream into a saucepan with the bread crumbs and warm on the stove. Stir in the salt, pepper, lemon juice, onion juice and parsley. Bring to a quick boil and mash in the salmon. Pour this hot mixture over the beaten egg yolks and stir lightly. Fill well buttered cups 2/3 full and set them in a pan of boiling water. Bake in a moderate oven (350 degrees) for 15 minutes, or until firm. Serve with Hollandaise sauce. Of course the cups can be deleted and the mixture can be baked in a well-buttered baking pan. General Lee sometimes enjoyed it even more with fine bread crumbs sprinkled all over the top before baking.

French Veronique—A Ruffin Household Special

3 pound frying chicken, cut up
2 tablespoons flour
1/2 teaspoon salt
1/2 teaspoon pepper
1/4 cup peanut oil
1/2 cup dry white wine
1/3 cup orange juice
2 tablespoons honey
1 tablespoon parsley
2 tablespoons orange peel, slivered
1 cup white grapes, halved

Roll the chicken pieces in a wooden mixing bowl containing a mixture of the flour, salt and 1/4 teaspoon of the pepper. Put the peanut oil into a cast iron skillet and heat. When very hot, drop in the chicken pieces and fry until brown on all sides. Stir in the wine, orange juice, honey, parsley and the remaining 1/4 teaspoon pepper. Cover the skillet and allow to simmer for 35 minutes, stirring occasionally. Lastly, add the slivered orange peel and continue simmering for another 15 minutes. Lay the chicken pieces on a large platter. Then add the grapes to the gravy and simmer, stirring constantly, for 3 minutes. Pour gravy over the chicken on the platter and serve immediately. This recipe feeds 5 people.

Edmund Ruffin, a Virginian born in 1794, gained fame for having fired the first shot against Fort Sumter on April 14, 1861.

EDMUND RUFFIN.

Beauregard's Old Fashioned Pound Cake

2/3 cup butter
2 cups flour
1 teaspoon baking powder
1/8 teaspoon salt
1 cup eggs
1 1/2 cups sugar
1/2 teaspoon nutmeg
2 tablespoons orange juice
1 teaspoon brandy

Cream the butter with the flour in a large wooden mixing bowl. In a separate bowl, add the baking powder and salt to the eggs and beat until light and fluffy. Add the sugar gradually and the nutmeg. Beat well. Put all of this into the bowl with the creamed flour and using a wooden spoon, stir until everything is blended thoroughly. Add the orange juice and brandy, stirring with long, light strokes. Turn this into a buttered and floured shallow cake tin. Bake in a moderate oven (350 degrees) for 1 hour.

General Pierre Beauregard (1818-1893) had a special liking for this pound cake. He was in charge of the Confederate troops that started the Civil War by firing on Fort Sumter in 1861. He fought and lost in the defense of Charleston against Sherman's forces in 1863.

Hampton's Homemade Plantation Biscuits

2 cups flour
1/3 cup butter
1/2 teaspoon salt
3/4 cup sour milk
1/2 teaspoon baking soda

Sift the flour with the salt in a wooden mixing bowl. Cut in the butter with a fork until the mixture is as fine as corn meal. In a separate bowl combine the sour milk and the baking soda until the baking soda is completely dissolved. Stir this into the flour mixture and continue to stir until a soft dough is formed. Take out of the mixing bowl and knead lightly on a floured surface for 1 minute. Roll out to a 1/4 inch thick sheet and cut with a floured biscuit cutter. Place each biscuit on a greased baking sheet. Bake in a very hot oven (450 degrees) for 12 minutes. This old recipe makes 1-1/2 dozen marvelous Dixie soda biscuits. It originated with the family of Wade Hampton in South Carolina.

In 1860 Hampton was considered to be one of the richest planters in the South, and he owned the largest number of slaves in the state. He was wounded in the first battle of Bull Run, and at Gettysburg, was wounded three more times.

WADE HAMPTON.

The Gatling Family Recipe for Salad Dressing

Richard Jordan Gatling was the man who, in 1861, conceived the idea of his revolving battery gun. Subsequently, 12 were manufactured and first used by General Butler in Virginia. In 1866, the Gatling gun was officially adopted by the government. This recipe for salad dressing was composed by his mother:

Two boiled potatoes, strained through a kitchen sieve,
   Softness and smoothness to the salad give;
Of mordant mustard take a single spoon—
   Distrust the condiment that bites too soon;
Yet deem it not, thou man of taste, a fault,
   To add as much as a double quantity of salt.
Four times the spoon with oil of Lucca crown,
   And twice with vinegar procured from the town;
True taste requires it, and your poet begs,
   The pounded yellow of two well-boiled eggs.
Let onions' atoms lurk within the bowl,
   And, scarce suspected, animate the whole;
And lastly, in the flavored compound toss,
   A magic spoonful of anchovy sauce.
Oh, great and glorious! oh, herbaceous meat!
   'Twould tempt the dying anchorite to eat.
Back to the world he'd turn his weary soul,
   And plunge his fingers in the salad bowl.

Authentic Recipes of Plantation Mammys

Cora Belle, a cook on a North Carolina plantation, was once asked how she cooked. She responded: "Lordy, honey, Ah don' eggzactly know. Ah jes' flings in and stirs and stirs and tasteses." As to making her marvelous gingerbread, she offered: "Ah takes a cup o' sugar, an' a cup o' flour, an' a gullup' o' molasses, an' jes' as many eggs as your Mama will gimme."

A favorite plantation dish was always served on New Year's Day to bring good luck throughout the upcoming year. It was called "Hoppin' John," and consisted of a slab of bacon cooked with black-eyed peas, rice and marrow bones. This was eaten with a huge slice of cornbread.

When cotton pickin' time rolled around, the plantation cook stocked up, loaded up, and headed out with the slaves. He sometimes awarded himself the luxury of a tarpaulin shelter. And often it was a lunch of pintos, collard greens and ham hocks over a quick fire, right out in the weather. George Washington Jones of the Hampton Plantation in South Carolina was typical of his profession—he turned out some real mealtime delights.

Authentic Plantation Spider Cake

Such cake as the name declares, is always baked in a spider. That's a cast iron frying pan with a short handle. Beat a few eggs pretty lightly and add a cup each of sweet milk and sour milk. Stir in your cornmeal and a handful of flour. Also use some sugar, some salt and a little soda. Beat the day lights out of it all and dump it in the spider, which should be greased and hot as the dickens. After the batter is in the frying pan, pour some more sweet milk over it, but don't try to stir it any more. Bake it in a hot oven, then put it on a plate, but don't break it.

Authentic Plantation Spider Cake

2 cups milk
1 teaspoon salt
2 cups corn meal
1/2 cup flour
2 tablespoons butter

Beat the eggs and sugar together in a large wooden mixing bowl. Dissolve the baking soda in the sour milk. Then add the sour milk, 1 cup of the unsoured milk and the salt. Stir lightly. Now gradually blend in the corn meal and the flour. Continue stirring *(do not beat)* the ingredients until everything is well blended. Put a cast iron skillet on the stove and when it is hot, melt in the butter. Turn the skillet so that the butter will run up on the sides. Pour the batter into the hot skillet and smooth over the top. Then slowly pour the other cup of unsoured milk over this, *but do not stir it in.* Place the skillet in the oven and bake at 425 degrees for about 25 minutes. When done, there will be a tasty streak of custard running through the cake. Cut into triangles and serve.

2 eggs
1/4 cup sugar
1 teaspoon baking soda
1 cup sour milk

Salt Cured Ham and Cider—A Plantation Favorite

Use a small lean salt cured ham. Wash the ham thoroughly in lukewarm water. Then soak the ham overnight in a large pot of cold water. Wipe dry the next morning and sprinkle over the flesh side a mixture of:

 2 tablespoons onion, chopped fine
 1/2 teaspoon mace
 2 tablespoons cinnamon
 2 tablespoons allspice
 1/2 teaspoon cloves

Make a paste using 2 cups flour mixed with water and carefully pat this all over the flesh side of the ham. Pack it down close to the skin area. Put the ham, skin side down, in a large roasting pan. Now you will need the following:

 8 cups cider
 1/2 teaspoon pepper
 1/2 teaspoon paprika

Blend these ingredients in a wooden mixing bowl and then pour into the roasting pan. Cover and bake in a moderate oven (350 degrees) for 2 hours. Baste every 20 minutes with the liquor in the bottom of the pan. At the end of 2 hours, remove the cover and allow the ham to cook for 2 more hours. When done, take the ham from the roasting pan and carefully scrape off all of the paste. Cut off all the skin at this time. Brush the skin side with a beaten egg and dust it thickly with bread crumbs and parsley. Skim off the grease from the cider in the bottom of the pan and throw away. Pour the cider into a saucepan and bring to a boil. Meanwhile, put the ham back in the pan and bake in a quick oven (450 degrees) until it browns. Continue simmering the liquor in the saucepan until there are only 2 cups left. Put this in a gravy bowl. When the ham is nicely browned, take it from the oven and serve on a large platter in a bed of watercress. Eat with the gravy.

Potato Puffs
on the Old Plantation

4 cups potatoes, mashed
1/4 teaspoon salt
1/4 teaspoon celery salt
1 tablespoon parsley
1/2 cup milk, hot
1 tablespoon butter, melted
1 egg, well beaten,
1 1/2 teaspoons baking powder

Put the mashed potatoes into a wooden mixing bowl and add the salt, celery salt, parsley, milk and butter. Beat thoroughly with a wooden spoon. Add the beaten egg and baking powder and stir until blended. Heap this mixture in a rough pile on a buttered baking pan. Bake in a moderate oven (350 degrees) for 10 minutes, or until puffed and browned. Serve while hot.

Flannel Cakes as
Prepared on the Plantation

1 cup flour
4 teaspoons baking powder
1 1/2 teaspoons salt
1 cup corn meal
1 egg, well beaten
2 cups milk
2 tablespoons butter, melted

Sift the flour with the baking powder and salt in a large wooden mixing bowl. Add the corn meal and stir until blended. In a separate bowl combine the beaten egg, milk and melted butter. Pour this into the dry ingredients and stir gently until well blended. Drop by large spoonfuls on a hot griddle greased with butter. When the flannel cakes puff and bubble, turn once and brown on the other side. Serve hot with maple syrup. This recipe makes 18 delightful flannel cakes, an oldtime favorite on frosty mornings.

Douglass's Best Molasses Candy Recipe

2 cups molasses
1 tablespoon vinegar
2 tablespoons butter
1/2 teaspoon baking powder
1 teaspoon vanilla

Put the molasses, vinegar and butter into a saucepan and bring to a boil. Stir continuously and boil until the mixture gets brittle when dropped into cold water. Then take off the stove and stir in the baking powder and vanilla. Pour into a buttered pan and set aside to cool. When nearly cold, pull until it looks glossy. Cut into small pieces and lay on a buttered dish or wrap in waxed paper. This old recipe makes 1 pound of delicious molasses candy.

Frederick Douglass (1817-1895) was a mulatto son of a slave mother who secretly taught himself to read and write. He fled from slavery at the age of 21, and later became the agent of the Massachusetts Anti-slavery Society. He authored *Narrative of My Experiences in Slavery* (1844) and *My Bondage and My Freedom* (1855).

FREDERICK DOUGLASS.

Old Fashioned Sweet Potato Pone

2 cups sweet potatoes, grated
1 cup milk
1 teaspoon ginger
2 tablespoons brown sugar
2 tablespoons butter, melted
1 1/2 cups flour
1 teaspoon salt
4 teaspoons baking powder

Put the grated sweet potatoes in a large wooden mixing bowl and add the milk, ginger, brown sugar and melted butter. Beat thoroughly. In a separate bowl, sift together the flour, salt and baking powder. Sift again. Then add this to the ingredients in the first bowl. Beat hard for 2 minutes and turn into a buttered baking pan. Bake in a moderate oven (350 degrees) for 45 minutes. Serve while hot and still in the baking pan. This is a spoon bread and should always be eaten as soon as it is taken from the oven. This recipe makes enough to feed 6 people.

Ham Croquettes—Plantation Style

1 cup ham, chopped fine
1/2 cup potatoes, mashed
1/2 teaspoon parsley
1/4 teaspoon salt
1/8 teaspoon pepper
1 egg
1 teaspoon baking powder

Blend all of the ingredients in a wooden mixing bowl. Shape into small balls and roll in dry bread crumbs. Deep fry in a skillet of hot grease. This recipe makes enough to serve 4 people. It was a favorite on Mississippi plantations and usually served with buttered peas or asparagus tips.

Old Plantation Stew with Dumplings

2 pounds beef, cut up in 1 inch cubes
2 cups carrots, cut up
2 cups onions, cut up
4 cups potatoes, cut up
1 cup tomatoes, cut up
1 tablespoon salt
1/4 teaspoon pepper

Put the beef into a large cast iron kettle and cover with cold water. Bring to a boil and allow to boil for 1-1/2 hours. Add the carrots and onions and boil for 15 more minutes. Add the potatoes, tomatoes, salt and pepper. Add more boiling water, if needed, to cover the vegetables. Boil for another 30 minutes. Now prepare the dumplings as follows:

> *1 cup flour*
> *2 teaspoons baking powder*
> *1/2 teaspoon salt*
> *1 teaspoon butter*
> *1/4 cup water, cold*

Sift together the flour, baking powder and salt into a wooden mixing bowl. Rub in the butter lightly with the fingers until all is well blended. Add the water and mix until the dough will hold together. Drop the dumplings by spoonfuls into the stew, cover, and allow to boil for 10 minutes. Place the meat and vegetables on a platter with the dumplings around the edge. Now take 1 tablespoon flour and blend it with a little cold water until it is free of lumps. Stir this into the liquor in the kettle and let boil for 3 minutes. Pour this over the stew on the platter and sprinkle with parsley.

Pork Fruit Cake—A Plantation Holiday Special

1 pound pork, ground
2 cups water, boiling
1 tablespoon baking soda
2 cups brown sugar
1 cup dark molasses
5 cups flour
1 tablespoon baking powder
1 tablespoon nutmeg
1 tablespoon allspice
1 tablespoon cinnamon

1 tablespoon cloves
1/2 teaspoon salt
2 cups black raisins
2 cups yellow raisins
4 cups currants
1 cup cherries, chopped

2 cups candied citron, shredded
1 cup nuts, chopped

Put the ground pork into a kettle with the boiling water and cook for 5 minutes. Set aside to cool. When cool, stir in the baking soda, brown sugar and dark molasses. Sift together the flour, baking powder, spices and salt. Add this to the mixture in the kettle. Lastly, stir in all the fruits and the nuts. Turn this mixture into a large buttered and floured cake tin. Bake in a moderate oven (350 degrees) for 3 hours. In the old days on the plantation, the cake pan would first be buttered and then lined with paper instead of floured.

Plantation Chicken and Tomato Delight

2 cups chicken, cooked and diced
2 cups water, boiling
2 cups tomatoes, stewed and drained
1/2 teaspoon salt
1/8 teaspoon pepper

1/2 small onion, chopped
1/2 teaspoon curry
1 cup rice
1/2 cup cream or
1/2 cup butter

Put the chicken in a saucepan with the boiling water. Cover and let simmer until the meat is extremely tender. Then take the chicken from the saucepan and skim the liquor. Add the tomatoes, salt, pepper, onion and curry. Stir while bringing to a boil. Add the rice and cook until the rice is soft. Put the chicken back in the saucepan and stir in the cream or butter. Serve while piping hot.

Scripture Cake as Made on the Plantation

4-1/2 cups of 1.Kings, IV:22
1 cup of Judges, V:25, last clause
2 cups of Jeremiah, VI:20
2 cups of Nahum, III:12
2 cups of 1.Samuel, XXX:12
1 cup of Numbers, XVII:8
2 tablespoons of 1.Samuel, XIV:25

Season to taste with II. Chronicles, IX:9; and pinch of Leviticus, II:13, last clause. Add 1/2 cup of Judges, IV:19 and 2 teaspoons of Amos IV:5. Follow Solomon's prescription for making a good boy, Proverbs, XXIII:14 ("Thou shalt beat him with a rod.") and you will have a good cake.

In modern terminology, the Scripture Cake can be made as follows:

1-1/4 cups flour
3-1/4 cups corn meal
1 cup butter
2 cups sugar
2 cups figs
2 cups raisins
1 cup almonds

2 tablespoons honey
1 teaspoon cinnamon
1 teaspoon nutmeg
1/8 teaspoon salt
1/2 cup milk
2 teaspoons yeast

Put all ingredients in a large wooden mixing bowl and beat well until completely blended. Grease and flour a 10-inch tube (bundt) pan and pour in mixture. Bake at 350 degrees for 1 hour.

The Original Midwestern Taste

While she was the hardest worker in the home, the woman rarely had to grind her own coffee. Hungry family members vied for her favor in a variety of ways. Some were known to fistfight for the privilege of cranking the grinder. The favorite coffee producer of the day was Arbuckle's, who packed a peppermint stick in every one pound bag. When the housewife was ready to open a new one, she'd holler, "Who wants the candy?" thereby reducing some of the toughest men who ever lived to a gang of quarrelling brats.

A delicious way of making a batter for frying fish is explained in an old midwestern cookbook: "As good a Batter as any, is just a little Ale and Flour beat up."

Salt pork was commonly fried and served for breakfast. And it was a mainstay provision for trappers, explorers and wagon trains passing through. It wouldn't spoil, it was easy to fix, and it was good to eat. A favorite dish was salt pork cooked in a large pot of split peas. "Trappers Fruit," another popular staple in the old midwest, was merely dried apples.

Clement Vallandigham's Chicken Croquettes
Put butter the size of a walnut in a saucepan over the fire. Fry in it chopped onion and flour. Add milk or water slowly, to the consistency of a sauce that will cling to the spoon. Season with salt and pepper. Put in it cooked chicken and mushrooms cut in small pieces but not chopped. Let cook a minute, then remove and stir in the yolks of eggs and some cooking wine, if desired. Pour into a well buttered deep plate, well rubbed with oil. Pour a few drops of oil on top to keep the chicken from hardening. Let cool several hours before breading and frying the same as fish croquettes.

Clement Vallandigham's Chicken Croquettes

3 egg yolks
1/4 cup cooking wine
1 teaspoon salad oil

Melt the butter in a large saucepan. Then sauté the onion until it turns brown. Blend in the flour. Now slowly add the milk or water and stir continuously until the sauce thickens. Add the salt, pepper, chicken and mushrooms. Stir well and bring to a boil. Immediately take the saucepan off the stove. Lastly, stir in the egg yolks and the wine. When well blended, pour the mixture into a bowl and sprinkle the salad oil on top. Set aside until completely cool. Then make thick patties and roll them in corn meal or bread crumbs. Deep fry in a cast iron skillet until nicely browned. Serve while very hot.

Clement L. Vallandigham was unpopular in Ohio when he openly showed sympathy for the Confederate cause. He was thought to be an enemy of his country and was arrested at his home on May 4, 1863, under a military order. He was charged with "treasonable conduct," and sentenced to "close confinement in a fortress for the remainder of the war."

1 tablespoon butter
1 tablespoon onion, chopped fine
1 tablespoon flour, heaping
2 cups milk or 2 cups water
1/2 teaspoon salt
1/8 teaspoon pepper
3 cups chicken, cooked and diced
1 cup mushrooms, cut up

Frederick Grant's Dutch Pepper Salad

1 head cabbage, grated
1 carrot, grated
1 onion, grated
1 green pepper, chopped
1/2 cup cream
1/2 cup apple cider vinegar
1/4 cup sugar
1 teaspoon salt

Blend the cabbage, carrot and onion in a wooden mixing bowl. Stir in the green pepper. In a separate bowl blend the cream, vinegar, sugar and salt. Pour this mixture over the vegetables in the other bowl. Stir thoroughly. Cover and chill for 3 hours to blend the flavors before serving cold. This recipe makes enough for 8 servings.

Frederick Dent Grant, the son of Ulysses S. Grant, was born in St. Louis, Missouri in 1850. He spent much time with his father during the Civil War, and later took part in the campaign on the frontier against the Indians. He was appointed a brigadier general by President McKinley.

FREDERICK DENT GRANT.

Midwestern Steamed Brown Bread

2 cups corn meal
1 cup graham flour
2 teaspoons baking powder
1 teaspoon salt
1/2 teaspoon baking soda
1 cup molasses
2 cups water, cold

Take a wooden mixing bowl and sift together the corn meal, graham flour, baking powder and salt. Repeat the sifting twice more. In a separate bowl stir the baking soda into the molasses and add the cold water. Blend well. Stir this mixture into the dry ingredients in the other bowl. Pour into a buttered baking dish and set in a large pan of water, cover, and allow to steam for 4 hours. Remove cover and place baking dish in a moderate oven (350 degrees) for 1/2 hour, or until top is dry and crusted. If a soft top is preferred, do not bake.

Fresh Corn Bread

2-1/2 cups fresh corn
1 cup flour
1 tablespoon sugar
1-1/2 teaspoons salt
2 teaspoons baking powder
1 egg, well beaten
1/4 cup butter, melted

Put the fresh kernels of corn into a large wooden mixing bowl. Sift together the flour, sugar, salt and baking powder. Repeat the sifting. Add this to the corn gradually, blending well. Stir in the beaten egg and then the melted butter. Pour into a buttered 8 inch square baking pan. Bake in a hot oven (400 degrees) for 30 minutes. This grand hot bread from the "Tall-corn Belt" may be enjoyed all year round. When sweet corn is out of season, use canned whole kernel corn. This unique corn bread is marvelous with broiled ham or chicken.

Gresham's Favorite Spinach Ring

4-1/2 quarts fresh spinach, ground
1 cup butter, melted
2 cups bread crumbs
1 tablespoon salt
1 teaspoon pepper
6 egg yolks, beaten
6 egg whites, beaten

Put the spinach into a large wooden mixing bowl and stir in the melted butter. Then add the bread crumbs, salt and pepper. Blend well. Stir in the beaten egg yolks. Lastly, carefully fold in the frothy egg whites. Pour the mixture into a nicely buttered baking mold. Place the mold in a pan of boiling water. Bake in a medium oven (350 degrees) for 20 to 30 minutes. Remove from mold and fill the center of the spinach ring with mushroom sauce or creamed hard-boiled eggs.

Walter Quinton Gresham (1832-1895) was a colonel in the 52nd Indiana Volunteers. This man was Postmaster General from 1882 to 1884; Secretary of the Treasury in 1884; and was later appointed Secretary of State by President Cleveland.

Prize Midwestern Meat Fold-overs of Long Ago

1/2 pound sausage, ground
1 cup chicken, chopped or
1 cup ham, chopped
1 cup rice, boiled
1 pimento, chopped
1 tablespoon Worcestershire sauce

2 eggs, separated
4 cups flour
1 teaspoon salt
1 teaspoon garlic powder
1/2 teaspoon pepper
2 teaspoons baking powder
6 tablespoons butter
3/4 cup water

Put the sausage meat into a hot cast iron skillet and fry slightly. Then stir in the chicken or ham and cook until everything is done. Stir in the rice, pimento and Worcestershire sauce. Take the skillet from the stove and blend in one beaten egg yolk. Lastly, fold in the frothy egg white. Set aside and sift together the flour, salt, garlic powder, pepper and baking powder in a wooden mixing bowl. Add the butter and cut with a fork into the flour mixture. Stir in the water and blend until a stiff dough is formed. Knead lightly for 1 minute. Lay the dough on a floured surface and roll out to 1/4 inch thick. Cut into pieces the size of a saucer. Put 2 tablespoons of the meat mixture in the center of each piece of dough. Wet the edges and then fold over and press the edges together with a fork. Brush each with some of the other egg yolk. Lay on a buttered baking tin and bake in a hot oven (425 degrees) for 10 minutes, or until a nice golden color. Serve while hot. This recipe makes 10 delightful fold-overs.

Cushing's Fabulous Shrimp Fantasy

1 cup peanut oil
1/2 cup coconut, flaked
1/3 cup bread crumbs
3 tablespoons parsley
1 tablespoon garlic, minced

1 teaspoon salt
1/4 teaspoon pepper
1/2 teaspoon paprika
2 pounds shrimp, raw
2/3 cup sherry wine

Put the peanut oil into a large wooden mixing bowl. Blend in the coconut, bread crumbs, parsley, garlic, salt, pepper and paprika. Take out 1/3 cup of the mixture and set aside as a topping. Put the raw shrimp into the bowl and stir lightly until each shrimp is nicely coated. Dump this mixture into a lightly buttered 1-1/2 quart casserole or baking pan. Pour the wine over this and sprinkle with the 1/3 cup of the mixture previously set aside. Bake, uncovered, in a moderately quick oven (375 degrees) for 40 minutes. This recipe makes enough to serve 5 people.

William Barker Cushing (1843-1900) enjoyed this delightful shrimp dish many times during his lifetime. He was a top rated naval officer during the Civil War and was notable for the destruction of the Confederate ram *Albemarle*, at Plymouth, North Carolina. He was a midwesterner who became famous and then forgotten with the passage of time.

WILLIAM BARKER CUSHING.

Shepherd's Pie

1-1/2 pounds lamb
8 cups water, cold
1 cup onions, sliced
1/2 cup carrots, diced
2 teaspoons salt
1/8 teaspoon pepper
2 tablespoons flour
4 cups potatoes, mashed
2 tablespoons paprika
2 tablespoons parsley

Put the meat and cold water into a large cast iron kettle, bring to a boil and allow to simmer for 1 hour. Then add the onions, carrots, salt and pepper. Simmer until tender. Remove 4 cups of the liquor from the kettle and set aside for making soup at a later time. Now stir the flour into the liquor remaining in the kettle and let this boil for 5 minutes. Put the mashed potatoes around the edge of a large platter. Place the meat and vegetables in the center. Dust with paprika and bake in a moderately hot oven (375 degrees) for 10 minutes, or until browned. Sprinkle with parsley and serve while hot. This recipe feeds 6 people.

Salmon and Tomato—
A Real Midwestern Treat

2 cups salmon, flaked
1 cup tomatoes, stewed
1 tablespoon butter, melted
1 teaspoon garlic powder
1/4 teaspoon salt
1/8 teaspoon pepper
1/2 teaspoon baking powder
1/2 cup bread crumbs

Take a wooden mixing bowl and blend together the salmon, tomatoes, butter, 1/2 teaspoon of the garlic powder, salt, pepper and baking powder. Turn this mixture into a well buttered loaf pan. Dust the top with the rest of the garlic powder and then the bread crumbs. Bake in a moderate oven (350 degrees) for 20 minutes. Serve while hot, or chill, slice and fry.

Roast Goose with Apple Dressing and Gravy

1 Goose (10 to 12 pounds)
1 tablespoon bacon grease
2 tablespoons onions, chopped fine
4 cups apples, chopped fine
4 cups bread crumbs
1 teaspoon salt
1/8 teaspoon pepper
1/2 teaspoon nutmeg
1/8 teaspoon paprika
1 egg, well beaten
2 tablespoons parsley

Put the bacon grease into a skillet and add the onions. Sauté until the onions are yellow. Add the apples and fry until soft. Cover the bread crumbs with water, then remove and press out all the water. Put the bread crumbs in with the onions and apples. Stir in the salt, pepper, nutmeg and paprika. Lastly, add the beaten egg and parsley. Blend well until thoroughly cooked.

Now take the goose and wipe the inside with a damp cloth. Sprinkle well with salt and pepper. Put in the apple dressing and sew up. Push back the skin and cut off the neck. Set aside until later, along with the heart, liver, gizzard and wing tips. In the skin put two apples which have been pared and quartered. Place in a roasting pan breast up. Dust liberally with salt, pepper and flour. Put in a hot oven (425 degrees) for 2 hours, or until browned. Baste often while roasting with 2 cups cold water. When browned, turn the breast side down and roast for another 2 hours. Baste four times with cold water. Ten minutes before serving, turn breast side up. Remove the liquor from the roasting pan and make the gravy as follows:

Goose neck, wing tips, heart, liver and gizzard
1 teaspoon onion, chopped fine
1 teaspoon salt
1/8 teaspoon pepper
2 tablespoons flour

Put the neck, wing tips, heart, liver and gizzard into a saucepan and cover with water. Boil until tender. Take the liquor from the roasting pan and add enough stock from the boiled giblets to make 3 cups. Chop the giblets. Add them and the onion, salt and pepper to the gravy mixture. Blend the flour with a little cold water and stir it in. Allow to boil for 3 minutes.

Eggplant Salad

2 pounds eggplant
2 tablespoons salt
1 cup flour
3/4 teaspoon pepper
1 cup flour
1 cup cooking oil
1/4 cup vinegar
1/3 cup onion, chopped
1 garlic clove, crushed
2 tablespoons pimento, chopped
2 tablespoons olives, chopped

Slice the unpeeled eggplant into 1/2 inch thick slices. Sprinkle with salt and set aside for 15 minutes. Blend the flour and pepper in a wooden mixing bowl. Coat each slice of eggplant with this flour mixture. Heat 1/2 cup of the cooking oil in a cast iron skillet. When hot, sauté the eggplant slices until golden brown. Now place each eggplant slice in a buttered shallow baking pan. Combine the remaining 1/2 cup cooking oil with the vinegar, onion, garlic, pimento and olives. Blend thoroughly and pour this over the eggplant slices.

Allow to chill and marinate 2 hours in the refrigerator. Then serve with a garnish of sliced hard-boiled eggs and ripe olives. This old recipe feeds 6 people.

Almond and Raisin Bread

1/2 cup brown sugar
3/4 cup water, hot
1/2 cup molasses
3/4 cup cream or
3/4 cup milk
1 cup flour
3 teaspoons baking powder
1 teaspoon salt
1/2 teaspoon baking soda
2 cups graham flour
1 tablespoon butter, melted
1/4 cup raisins, chopped
1 cup almonds, chopped

Put the brown sugar in a large wooden mixing bowl and pour in the hot water. Stir until the sugar is dissolved. Add the molasses and the cream or milk. Blend well. In a separate bowl sift together the flour, baking powder, salt and baking soda. Stir these into the milk mixture in the other bowl. Now stir in the graham flour. Add the melted butter, raisins and almonds. Blend everything thoroughly. Turn into a well-buttered loaf pan. Bake in a moderate oven (350 degrees) for 1-1/2 hours. This recipe makes 1 medium-sized loaf of delightful bread.

Midwestern Spicy Chicken

2 large chickens, halved
2 large onions, chopped
2 green peppers, diced
2 large tomatoes, chopped
2 teaspoons salt
1 tablespoon curry powder
1 tablespoon coriander
1 tablespoon cumin
1 teaspoon turmeric
1/2 teaspoon cinnamon
3/4 teaspoon garlic powder
1 teaspoon pepper
1/2 cup butter, melted
2 cups water, boiling

Put the chicken halves into a shallow baking pan. Sprinkle with the onion, green peppers, tomatoes, salt and all the spices. Pour in the melted butter. Turn chicken a number of times to mix the pieces with all the ingredients. Cover and allow to marinate in the refrigerator for 3 hours, or it is even better to leave it overnight. Lastly, stir in the boiling water and bake in a moderately hot oven (375 degrees) for 50 minutes. Most midwesterners enjoy this best when served with hot cooked rice, and garnished with slices of fresh tomato, celery stalks and green pepper rings.

John Alexander Logan's Fried Tomatoes

JOHN ALEXANDER LOGAN.

John Logan (1826-1886) was a private in a Michigan regiment at the battle of Bull Run in 1861. He later served in Congress from 1859 to 1862. Here is his poetic recipe:

If you would fry tomatoes right,
Select large fresh ones, clean and bright;
    Slice them thick as are your thumbs,
And roll them well in cracker crumbs;
    Add salt and pepper to the taste,
A little sugar too in haste;
    Then with a fire hot and bright,
Heat well your pan and do not slight,
    The lard and butter, lest it burn.
When brown on one side over-turn;
    And when at last, both sides are done,
Hot from the spider, give us one.

Presidential Parade of Favorites

One of our Presidents cared little for sugar. John Adams instructed his housekeeper to clean out pumpkins and set them outside for several cold evenings. The collected juices were then boiled down to a sugary syrup and used in its place at the Adams' dinner table.

James Buchanan actually collected the labels from packages of coffee which he redeemed for razors from a company in Pittsburgh, Pennsylvania. This may well have been the forerunner of today's popular trading stamps.

Two Presidents had definite ideas about food and health. Andrew Jackson often recommended the eating of rhubarb roots for protection against scurvy. And he was probably quite correct as the root is loaded with vitamins. Zachary Taylor believed coffee and tea were both marvelous as medicines. He advised the drinking of both to avoid gout and headaches.

George Washington owned a sago palm. Nutritious and wholesome starch made from this West Indian palm was used by his family.

Abe Lincoln's Favorite Almond White Cake
Cream one cup of butter and two cups of sugar lightly. Sift three cups of flour and two teaspoonsfull of baking powder together; then alternate with one cup of milk to the creamed mixture. Beat six egg whites until they form a stiff froth. To the first mixture add one cup of well floured chopped blanched almonds and then one teaspoonfull of vanilla. Now fold in the frothy egg whites to which has been added one-quarter teaspoonfull of salt. Pour the batter in three pans about eight or nine inches across, and bake in a moderate oven. Cover each layer with BOILED ICING to which has been added a half cup of blanched almonds.

Abe Lincoln's Favorite Almond White Cake

3 cups flour
2 teaspoons baking
    powder
1 cup blanched almonds,
    chopped fine
1 cup butter
2 cups sugar
1 teaspoon vanilla
1 cup milk
6 egg whites
1/4 teaspoon salt

Sift the flour and the baking powder 3 times in a large wooden mixing bowl. Then stir in the blanched almonds. Set this dry mixture aside and proceed to cream the butter and the sugar in a separate bowl. Now add the vanilla to this creamy blend. Then stir in the flour mixture and milk alternately until it is all used up. Set aside while beating the egg whites with the salt until stiff. Fold these egg whites carefully into the batter. Pour the batter into 3 round, well-greased and floured cake pans. Bake in a moderate oven (350 degrees) for about 20 minutes or until a straw comes out clean. To make Abe's favorite icing, it takes:

2 cups sugar
1/2 cup water, hot
2 egg whites
1/8 teaspoon cream of tartar
1/2 cup blanched almonds, chopped fine
1 teaspoon lemon juice

Blend the sugar and hot water in a saucepan and quickly bring this to a boil. Continue to boil until it strings, but *do not stir.* Beat the egg whites until stiff in a wooden mixing bowl. Slowly pour the sugar-water mixture into the stiffly beaten egg whites and blend well. Stir in the cream of tartar, blanched almonds and lemon juice. Beat thoroughly. When thick and smooth, spread between layers and on the top of the cooled cake. This boiled icing hardens rather quickly.

Lincoln ate this cake often before he married Mary Todd. He declared it to be the best he ever had. Mrs. Thomas Lincoln, Abe's stepmother, said: "Abe was a moderate eater. He sat down and ate what was set before him, making no complaint. He seemed careless about this."

Lobster Salad as Prepared for John Adams

Pick out all the meat from the body and claws of a cold boiled lobster. Mince the meat and blend with:

4 tablespoons cabbage, chopped fine
2 small onions, minced

Set this mixture aside while preparing the special dressing. For this the following ingredients are required:

4 eggs, hardboiled
2 tablespoons salad oil
1 teaspoon mustard
1 teaspoon salt
2 teaspoons sugar
1/2 teaspoon red pepper
1 teaspoon Worcestershire sauce
1 tablespoon vinegar

Put the egg yolks into a small mixing bowl and rub until they become a smooth paste. Use only a wooden spoon for this. In the days of John Adams they used a mortar and pestle. The yolks must be free of all lumps. Add gradually, rubbing all the time, all the other ingredients. Moisten with a little more vinegar if necessary. You should end up with 3/4 cup of dressing and it should be thin enough to pour over the lobster mixture. Pour this over the lobster and stir long and hard. The meat must be thoroughly impregnated with the dressing. All lobster salad should, according to Abigail, be eaten as soon as the dressing has been added. Garnish the salad with a chain of rings made by slicing the hardboiled egg whites. To make this salad as authentic as possible, the Worcestershire sauce should also be prepared as it was many long years ago by Abigail Adams. Make it as follows:

3 teaspoons red pepper
3 scallions, minced
4 cups vinegar
2 tablespoons catsup
3 anchovies, chopped fine

Thoroughly blend all of the above ingredients and rub them through a fine strainer. Put into a stone jar and set this in a pot of boiling water. Heat until the liquid in the jar is so hot you cannot keep your finger in it. Immediately strain and let stand in the jar, covered tightly, for 2 days, then put into bottles and seal until ready to use.

Boiled Custard of 1810—A James Madison Favorite

5 egg whites, stiffly beaten
2 teaspoons vanilla
1 tablespoon powdered sugar, heaping
2 egg whites

Heat the milk in a saucepan almost to boiling. Stir the sugar into the beaten egg yolks. Take the scalding milk from the stove. Instead of pouring the beaten egg yolks into this, put 2 tablespoons of the hot milk in with them. Beat well while doing this. Add more and more milk until there is no longer any danger of sudden curdling. Now stir in the stiffly beaten egg whites. Pour this mixture into the saucepan and boil gently until it becomes thick (10 to 15 minutes should suffice). Stir constantly while boiling. Now stir in the vanilla and pour the custard into heated glass cups. Whip the powdered sugar and 2 egg whites to a thick meringue. When the custard has cooled, pile a little of this on top of each cup. Dolly Madison garnished her custard with strawberry or cherry preserves, a bit of fresh melon, or a little jelly. It was carefully placed on top of the meringue for each cup.

4 cups milk
5 egg yolks, well beaten
6 tablespoons sugar

Zachary Taylor's Special Red Bean Soup

2 cups kidney beans
4 cups vegetable stock
1 tablespoon butter
1 tablespoon flour
1/2 teaspoon cloves

1/2 teaspoon cinnamon
1/2 teaspoon celery flakes
1/4 teaspoon curry powder
1 tablespoon salt
1 teaspoon black pepper
2 lemons, juice only

This is believed to be one of the very best bean soups known in the long-forgotten past. Put the beans into a cast iron kettle with 4 cups cold water. Bring to a boil for 2 minutes and then remove from the stove. Let stand overnight. Then bring to a boil again and allow to simmer for 1-1/2 hours. Then strain the beans into the vegetable stock and heat. Meanwhile blend the butter and flour in a small wooden mixing bowl until it is a smooth cream. Then add this to the soup in the kettle, and stir in the cloves, cinnamon, celery flakes, curry powder, salt and pepper. The lemon juice is to be blended in the soup just before serving. Zachary Taylor also enjoyed this soup when made with lima beans.

James Monroe's Delicate Fritters

1 cup flour
1-1/2 teaspoons baking powder
2 tablespoons cornstarch
1/4 teaspoon salt

4 tablespoons sugar
1 egg, separated
1/3 cup milk
1 tablespoon olive oil

Blend the flour, baking powder, cornstarch, salt and sugar in a wooden mixing bowl and sift 3 times. Beat the yolk and the white of the egg separately. Add the beaten egg yolk and milk alternately to the flour mixture. Then add the olive oil and beat until smooth. Finally fold in the stiffly beaten egg white. Drop by large wooden spoonfuls into plenty of hot, but not smoking, cooking oil. Allow to fry until golden brown and turn once. Drain out with a skimmer, and lay the fritters on absorbent paper or a clean cloth. Dust with powdered sugar and serve at once.

Elizabeth Monroe used this batter recipe for plain fritters and for fruit and sweet fritters of all kinds. In using vegetables or shellfish, she omitted the sugar. She thinned the batter slightly with milk when she used it with any filling such as apples, clams or oysters. This recipe is sufficient for 10 large fritters.

President Grant's Mushroom-Chicken Loaf

2-1/2 cups chicken, cooked and diced
1/2 cup mushrooms, cooked
1 cup bread crumbs, soft
1-1/2 teaspoons salt
1/4 teaspoon paprika
1/4 teaspoon celery flakes
2 egg yolks
1-1/4 cups milk
2 tablespoons butter, melted
2 egg whites, stiffly beaten

Julia Dent Grant blended all of the following in a large wooden mixing bowl: chicken, mushrooms, bread crumbs, salt, paprika, celery flakes, egg yolks, milk and butter. She let it stand for 10 minutes and then folded in the egg whites. The mixture was then poured into a buttered loaf pan and baked in a moderate oven (350 degrees) for 1 hour. It was always served with a special mushroom sauce made as follows:

> *3/4 cup mushrooms*
> *3/4 cup cream*
> *4 tablespoons butter*
> *1/4 teaspoon mace*

1/4 teaspoon nutmeg
1/2 teaspoon salt
1 teaspoon flour

Put the fresh mushrooms into a saucepan and barely cover with water. Cook until tender and drain the mushrooms, but do not press them. Add the cream, butter and seasonings. Simmer and stir continuously until the mixture begins to thicken. Then wet the flour in a little cold milk and stir it in. Bring to a quick boil and pour into a gravy boat. Serve while steaming hot.

Raspberry Royal Enjoyed by the Polk Family

4 cups ripe raspberries
4 cups cider vinegar
2 cups sugar
2 cups brandy

Put the fresh raspberries into a stone jar and pour the cider vinegar over them. Stir in the sugar and pound the raspberries to a paste with a wooden pestle, or mash them with a wooden spoon. Let this mixture stand in the sun for 4 hours. Then strain through cheesecloth. Squeeze out all of the juice. Blend the brandy with this strained berry juice. Pour into sterilized bottles and seal.

President Polk would stir 2 tablespoons of this into a tumbler of ice water when he wished a refreshing drink. It was his favorite while relaxing. Polk used to lay the bottles on their sides in his cellar. They were then covered with sawdust until needed.

John Quincy Adams' Fancy Frosted Tea Cookies

3/4 cup butter
1/2 cup sugar
2 small eggs, beaten
1/2 teaspoon almond extract
3 cups flour
1 teaspoon baking powder
1/2 cup almonds, ground

Cream the butter and the sugar together in a wooden mixing bowl. Then stir in the beaten eggs and the almond extract. Sift the flour and baking powder together, blend in the almonds and add this mixture to that in the bowl. Knead lightly and roll out on a floured surface. Cut out your cookies with a plain round cutter and lay them on greased baking pans. Now prepare the icing as follows:

1-3/4 cups powdered sugar
1 egg white
1 teaspoon lemon juice
1/2 cup almonds, shredded

Sift the powdered sugar into a wooden mixing bowl and stir in the egg white and lemon juice. Beat for 15 minutes. If too thick, add a very little more egg white.

Spread some of this icing on each cookie and sprinkle with the shredded almonds. Bake in a moderate oven (350 degrees) for 10 minutes. This recipe makes 50 delightful cookies.

Stewed Beets—
As Eaten by Martin Van Buren

12 medium beets
1 scallion, minced
1/2 teaspoon parsley

1/8 teaspoon salt
1/8 teaspoon pepper
2 tablespoons butter, melted
2 tablespoons vinegar

Put the young, sweet beets into a kettle of boiling water. Allow to slowly simmer until nearly done. Then drain well. Skin and slice the beets. Put the slices into a saucepan with the rest of the ingredients. Let it all simmer for 20 minutes. Shake the saucepan now and then to prevent burning the mixture. Serve while hot with the saucepan gravy poured over them.

William Henry Harrison's
Special Oyster Dish

1 large loaf French bread
3 dozen oysters, fried
1/4 cup butter, melted

Carefully slice the top edge off a loaf of fresh French bread. Dig out most of the soft inner bread. Wipe the loaf, inside and out, and the piece sliced off the top, with the melted butter. Put the loaf into the oven and leave it until slightly browned. Take from the oven and pack the fried oysters down in the loaf. Place the top back on the loaf, lay on a buttered cookie tin, and set back in a moderate oven (350 degrees). Leave this until the bread appears to be nicely browned all over. Serve immediately with a garnish of catsup or a relish of your choice. Harrison most enjoyed this dish with sweet pickle relish.

Rachel Jackson's Famed Grape Salad

2 pounds green grapes, seedless
1 cup celery, chopped
1/2 cup sweet cucumber pickles, chopped

Cut the grapes into halves and blend with the celery and the cucumber pickles. Set aside while preparing the dressing:

2 eggs, well beaten
1 cup cider vinegar
1/2 cup sugar
1/2 teaspoon salt
1/2 teaspoon pepper
1 teaspoon mustard
1 tablespoon butter, well rounded
1 teaspoon cornstarch, wet with cream
3/4 cup cream

Put all of these ingredients, except for the cream, into a saucepan. Stir until it comes to a boil. Set aside while stirring occasionally, until it cools. Beat the cream with a little sugar and stir in last. Pour the dressing into a large serving bowl. Add the grape salad mixture and blend them together. Serve when chilled. This was a favorite of President Andrew Jackson for many years.

Franklin Pierce's Clam Soup Poem

First catch your clams—along the ebbing edges,
 Of saline coves you'll find the little wedges,
With backs up, lurking in the sandy bottom;
 Pull in your iron rake and lo! You've got 'em!
Take thirty large ones. Put a basin under,
 And cleave, with knife their stony jaws asunder;

Add water (three quarts) to the native liquor,
 Bring to a boil, and, by the way, the quicker
It boils the better, if you do it cutely.
 Now add the clams chopped up and minced
  minutely,
Allow a longer boil of just three minutes,
 And while it bubbles, quickly stir within its
Tumultuous depths where still the mollusks
  mutter,
 Four tablespoons of flour and four of butter,
A pint of milk, some pepper to your notion,
 And clams need salting although born of the
  ocean.
Remove from the fire; if much boiled they will
  suffer—
 You'll find that a wood spoon is not much
  tougher.
After 'tis off add three fresh eggs, well beaten,
 Stir once more, and 'tis ready to be eaten.
Fruit of the wave! O, dainty and delicious!
 Food for the gods! Ambrosia for Apicius!
Worthy to thrill the soul of Venus,
 Or titillate the palate of Silenus.

America's Earliest Cooking School

Miss Juliet Corson opened and ran the nation's first cooking school for women in New York City of 1874. Her course was aptly called "Demonstrative Lessons in Cookery."

Frances E. Owens was one of Juliet Corson's star pupils. She later went on to write *Mrs. Owens' Cook Book and Useful Hints for the Household*. This particular book was published in 1882, and in it she credits many of her fine recipes to "friends living in all sections . . . choice cooking recipes and hints for the household, culled from practical every day experience." Other recipes in her book were attributed to Miss Corson's popular cooking classes.

The first recipe given is exactly as originally presented in Miss Corson's "Demonstrative Lessons in Cookery." The rest have been updated from the originals for more practical use by modern cooks.

Miss Juliet Corson's Original Hot Egg Salad
4 tablespoons Salad Oil made hot. Break your eggs into it, and stir a little. Season with salt and pepper. Turn out as soon as it hardens a trifle, sprinkle over the top a little chopped cucumber, same of grated lemon rind, same of lemon juice and some salad oil.

Miss Juliet Corson's Original Hot Egg Salad

4 tablespoons salad oil
3 eggs
1/2 teaspoon salt
1/4 teaspoon pepper

1 tablespoon cucumber, chopped fine
1 tablespoon lemon rind, grated
1 tablespoon lemon juice

Heat 1 tablespoon salad oil in a cast iron skillet. Then break the eggs in the pan and season with salt and pepper. Stir constantly as the eggs fry. Turn them as soon as they stiffen enough. Sprinkle the eggs with cucumber, lemon rind, lemon juice and 3 tablespoons salad oil. Take off the stove and cover the skillet. Let it set for 1 minute before serving.

Candied Sweet Potatoes— From Corson's Cookery Classes

6 medium sweet potatoes
1 cup brown sugar
1/2 cup water
1/2 cup butter, melted
1/4 teaspoon salt

Put the sweet potatoes into a kettle of cold water and bring to a boil. Allow to cook until done. Set aside to cool. Meanwhile, put the brown sugar and water in a small saucepan and bring to a boil. Allow to simmer for 5 minutes to make a syrup. Then add the butter and salt. Peel the cold sweet potatoes and cut in slices. Lay in a buttered baking pan. Pour the syrup mixture over the sweet potatoes and bake in a moderate oven (350 degrees) for 1 hour. Baste frequently while baking. The sweet potatoes should look transparent when done.

Mr. Blaine's Favorite Cabbage Soup

4 quarts water
3 pounds beef, cut into 1 inch cubes
1 pound beef soup bones
1 garlic clove
1 bay leaf
2 tablespoons parsley
1 teaspoon dill weed
1 tablespoon salt
1 teaspoon pepper
3 carrots, cut in 1/2 inch pieces
2 cups onions, sliced thin
1 medium head cabbage, chopped
2 small turnips, diced
3 stalks celery, cut in 1 inch pieces
3 large potatoes, peeled and diced
3-1/2 cups tomatoes, stewed and chopped

Put the water in a large cast iron kettle and add the beef and soup bones. Put a toothpick through the garlic clove and add it to the pot. Then add the bay leaf, parsley, dill, salt and pepper. Bring to a boil and allow to simmer for 2 hours. Skim off the foam and excess grease as they rise to the surface. Remove the bones, garlic and bay leaf. Add the carrots, onions, cabbage, turnips and celery. Let this all simmer for another 30 minutes. Lastly, add the potatoes and tomatoes. Cook for 30 minutes more. Serve while piping hot. Garnish with some fresh minced parsley and serve with a bowl of sour cream on the side. This recipe makes 7 quarts of delicious soup.

James Gillespie Blaine (1830-1893) was a good friend of Juliet Corson. He was one of the founders of the Republican Party, and in 1856 was a delegate to the first Republican National Convention, which nominated Fremont for the Presidency.

Mousse of Crab Meat

2 tablespoons gelatine
1 cup water, cold
1 cup water, boiling
1 cup mayonnaise
1 cup cream, stiffly whipped
2 cups crab meat, flaked
3 tablespoons pimento

Put the gelatine in a small bowl with the cold water and allow to soak for 5 minutes. Then stir in the boiling water and let cool. Slowly blend in the mayonnaise and the whipped cream. Lastly, stir in the flaked crab meat. Pour this mixture into one large mold or a group of individual molds. Set in refrigerator and leave for 3 hours or longer. Garnish with strips of pimento. Serve this mousse with sour cream dressing to be made as follows:

1 cup sour cream
2 tablespoons vinegar
1 clove garlic, diced
1 large cucumber, diced

Beat the sour cream until it begins to thicken. Stir in the vinegar, garlic and cucumber. Blend well and then chill before serving on top of the mousse.

Fat Rascals— A Juliet Corson Original

2 eggs, separated
5 teaspoons flour
1/2 cup milk
5 tablespoons cheese, grated
2 cups potatoes, mashed

Put the egg yolks into a wooden mixing bowl and beat until light and smooth. Stir in the flour, milk, cheese and mashed potatoes. Beat all of these ingredients until they are well blended and fluffy. Lastly, fold in the stiffly beaten egg whites. Drop by teaspoonfuls into a small kettle of hot cooking oil. Fry until nicely browned.

Miss Corson's Brown Sugar Fudge

2 cups brown sugar
1 cup sugar
3/4 cup milk
1 tablespoon butter
1/2 teaspoon vanilla
3/4 cup nuts, chopped

Combine the brown sugar, regular sugar and milk in a saucepan. Place on the stove and stir constantly until the mixture comes to a boil. Stir until the sugar is completely dissolved. Then continue to simmer without stirring. As soon as the mixture starts to thicken, begin testing by dropping a few drops into some cold water. The fudge is done when it forms a soft ball in the cold water. Put the saucepan in a larger pan of ice water and keep changing water until the fudge is cool enough to hold your hand on the bottom of saucepan. *Never beat fudge while hot.* Now add the butter and vanilla. Then, with a large wooden spoon, beat the fudge thoroughly in order to make it creamy. Lastly, add the nuts and beat the fudge until it loses its gloss. Pour into a 9 inch square, buttered baking pan or glass baking dish and set aside until ready to eat.

Corson's Prize Winning Liver Dish

1 pound liver, sliced
1/2 teaspoon salt
1/4 teaspoon pepper
1/4 cup flour
1/4 cup bacon grease
1 cup tomatoes, stewed
3 green peppers, chopped
6 small onions, chopped
2 cups water, boiling
1/2 teaspoon celery salt
1/2 teaspoon poultry seasoning
3 cups cooked noodles

Put the liver into a wooden mixing bowl and pour boiling water over this. Let stand for 5 minutes. Drain and wipe each slice dry. Dredge with the salt, pepper and flour. Meanwhile, put the bacon grease into a cast iron skillet and heat. When the grease is very hot, add the liver and fry until browned. Add the tomatoes, peppers, onions, boiling water, celery salt and poultry seasoning. Stir well and bring to a boil. Cover and allow to simmer for 45 minutes. Serve with the noodles. This recipe feeds 8 people.

Coffee Soufflé

3 tablespoons butter
3 tablespoons flour
3/4 cup coffee
1/4 cup cream
1/2 cup sugar
1/4 teaspoon salt
4 eggs, separated
1/2 teaspoon baking powder
1 teaspoon vanilla

Melt the butter in a saucepan and blend in the flour until smooth and pasty. Pour on gradually, while stirring constantly, the coffee, cream, sugar and salt. Stir and let simmer until smooth. Then beat the egg yolks and stir them into the mixture. Set aside to cool. When cold, beat the egg whites until they are frothy. Fold these in with the other ingredients. Now add the baking powder and vanilla. Blend well and pour into a nicely buttered baking pan. Bake in a moderately hot oven (375 degrees) for 25 minutes. While the soufflé is baking, prepare the sauce as follows:

2 egg yolks
1/4 cup sugar
1/8 teaspoon salt
1/2 cup strong coffee, hot
1 cup cream, whipped

Blend the egg yolks with the sugar in a wooden mixing bowl. Then stir in the salt and the coffee. Set aside to cool. When cold, fold in the whipped cream. Put this sauce on top of the soufflé when serving. This recipe feeds 4 people and it's delightfully rich.

Juliet Corson's Favorite Pepper Hash

12 green peppers, chopped fine
12 red peppers, chopped fine
16 onions, chopped fine
4 cups vinegar
2 teaspoons salt
1 cup sugar

Put the peppers and onions into a large pot and pour boiling water over them. Allow to stand for 5 minutes. Drain well and repeat the process. Meanwhile, put the vinegar, salt and sugar in a cast iron kettle and bring to a boil. Drain the peppers and onions. Add them to the boiling mixture and let simmer for 10 minutes. Pour into pint jars and seal until ready to use. This recipe makes 6 pints of relish.

Melt the butter in a cast iron skillet. Put in the oysters with their liquor and allow them to come to a boil. Quickly stir in the cream and pepper. Blend the flour with a little cold milk and add this. Let this mixture boil gently until the oysters curl. Remove the skillet from the stove and stir in the beaten egg yolks. Pour over a platter of toasted crackers and serve while steaming hot.

George Bancroft was an American historian and close friend of Juliet Corson.

Bancroft's Favorite Cooking School Oyster Fricassee

1 cup butter
2 quarts oysters
1 cup cream
1/2 teaspoon pepper
1 tablespoon flour
3 egg yolks, well beaten

GEORGE BANCROFT.

Frances E. Owens' Imperial Macaroni Delight

1 cup macaroni, uncooked
1/2 cup bread crumbs, soft
1/4 cup butter, melted
3 tablespoons red pepper, finely chopped
3 tablespoons green pepper, finely chopped
1-1/2 teaspoons onion, grated
1-1/2 teaspoons salt
1 teaspoon pepper
1 cup cheddar cheese, grated

1-1/2 cups milk, scalded
3 egg yolks, well beaten
3 egg whites, stiffly beaten

Put the macaroni in a small pot and cover with salted water. Bring to a boil and cook until tender. Take a large wooden mixing bowl and combine the bread crumbs, melted butter, red and green pepper, onion, salt, pepper and cheese. Blend well and stir in the scalded milk. Pour in the egg yolks and blend. Drain the macaroni and add to the mixture. Lastly, fold in the stiff egg whites. Pour all of this into a well-buttered baking pan and set in a larger pan of hot water. Bake in a moderate oven (350 degrees) for 40 to 45 minutes, or until firm. This recipe feeds 6 people.

The Boston Cooking School of 1879

The "Boston Cooking School" was started by Mary Lincoln in 1879, five years after Miss Corson's school opened in New York. Lincoln was also the school's first principal. *The Boston Cook Book* was published by this same lady in 1884. Her school of cookery later became famous under Fanny Farmer, a name we still find on many products today in our jet-age supermarkets.

Mary Lincoln's Special Corn Pancakes
Grate six large ears of corn, add to this the beaten yolks of two eggs, one cup of milk, one cup of flour, a little salt and pepper, and when well mixed stir in the stiffly beaten whites of the eggs. Bake on a hot griddle.

Mary Lincoln's Special Corn Pancakes

1 cup flour
1/2 teaspoon salt
1/8 teaspoon pepper
6 large ears of corn
2 egg yolks, beaten
1 cup milk
2 egg whites, beaten

Blend the flour, salt and pepper in a wooden mixing bowl and set aside. Meanwhile, grate the ears of corn and stir this into the dry flour mixture. Beat the egg yolks thoroughly. Now add the egg yolks and the milk to the corn and flour and stir until well blended. Beat the egg whites until they are stiff. Lastly, carefully fold in the beaten egg whites. Using 1/3 cup of this mixture per pancake, cook them in a heated, greased cast iron skillet until covered with bubbles. Turn pancakes and brown other side. Makes 12 small cakes, which can be eaten with syrup or plain as a delicious bread to accompany lentils, split peas, beans or soup. As a bread, it can also be prepared by pouring the mixture into the skillet and baking at 450 degrees for 20 minutes or until lightly browned.

Frying Pan Boiled Liver

4 slices bacon
1 medium onion, chopped
1 tablespoon flour
1 teaspoon powdered chili
1 pound beef liver, thin slices
2 cups tomatoes, stewed
1-1/2 cups whole kernel corn, drained
1 teaspoon salt

Put the slices of bacon into a frying pan and fry until crispy. Drain thoroughly and then break into small pieces. Now fry the onion in the bacon grease until tender. Blend the flour and the chili powder in a wooden mixing bowl and dip each slice of liver in this mixture. Put each slice into the frying pan and fry until lightly browned on each side. Lastly, add the bacon, tomatoes, corn and salt. Let this boil gently for 5 minutes, or until the liver is tender.

Snappy Corn Fondue Pudding

2 eggs
1/2 cup bread crumbs
1 tablespoon onion, finely chopped
1 tablespoon green pepper, chopped

1 cup cheese, shredded
2 cups corn, cream-style
1-1/2 teaspoons salt
1/2 teaspoon pepper
2/3 cup milk

Put the eggs into a wooden mixing bowl and beat well. Stir in the rest of the ingredients. Pour this mixture into a greased baking pan and set in a pan of hot water. Bake in a moderate oven (350 degrees) for 1 hour and 20 minutes, or until a knife inserted in the center comes out clean. This grand old recipe makes enough to serve 6 people.

Pork Tenderloin Bouquet

2 pounds pork roast, boneless
1 teaspoon salt
3/4 teaspoon oregano
1/2 teaspoon pepper
1 onion, chopped
1 garlic clove, minced
1 cup butter, melted
16 onions, small
4 carrots
1/3 cup flour, sifted
2 cups pork stock
4 potatoes, peeled
1 tablespoon butter, melted
2 tablespoons burgundy
2 teaspoons parsley

Cut the pork roast into 4 equal slices and sprinkle with the salt, oregano and pepper. Put the cup of melted butter in a large cast iron skillet and sauté the pork slices. Then take the pork slices and put them into a large baking pan. Add to this the onions and the carrots and set aside. Meanwhile, sauté the chopped onion and garlic in the skillet, and when done, stir in the flour, letting it cook until bubbly. Now add the pork stock to the skillet and stir until thick and smooth. Pour this mixture over the meat, carrots and onions in the baking pan. Bake this in a medium oven (350 degrees) for 50 minutes. While baking, boil the potatoes until soft. Drain them and then brown in butter using a small skillet. Put the potatoes around the pork and let it all bake for another 10 minutes. Serving this dish is truly an artistic masterpiece. Cut each slice of pork into 4 equal pieces. Do the same with the carrots. Lace the meat, carrots and onions in sequence on a skewer. Lastly, take the sauce from the baking pan and stir in the burgundy. Place the 4 skewers on a large platter and pour this wine sauce over them. Garnish with the potatoes and the parsley.

Lamb and Lentil Pottage

3-1/2 cups onions, sliced
1/2 cup cooking oil
1 pound lamb, ground
3 cups tomatoes, stewed
1-1/3 cups celery, diced
1 cup carrots, sliced
1 cup parsnips, diced
1 cup green pepper, diced
4 cups water
2 cups lentils
1 tablespoon salt
1/2 teaspoon pepper

Take a large pot and heat the cooking oil. Sauté the onions in this until they are soft. Then add in the ground lamb and cook until it browns nicely. Stir in the tomatoes, celery, carrots, parsnip and green pepper. Now add the water, lentils, salt and pepper. Continue cooking over a low heat for 1-1/2 hours, or until the lentils are tender. This recipe makes 8 delicious servings of soup. It is similar to "that red red pottage" of Biblical times, for which Esau sold his birthright.

Unusual Stuffed Peppers

4 medium size green peppers
1 small onion, diced
4 tablespoons butter, melted
1 cup split peas, cooked

1 cup ham, diced
1-1/4 cup bread crumbs, soft
1 egg, slightly beaten
1 teaspoon salt
1/4 teaspoon pepper
1/4 cup celery, diced

Carefully cut out the stem ends of the peppers and remove all the seeds. Put the peppers in a pot and cover with water. Add 1/2 teaspoon salt and bring to a boil. Wait 5 minutes and drain. Now cook the onion in 2 tablespoons of the butter until they are soft. Blend in the split peas, ham, 1 cup of the bread crumbs, beaten egg, salt, pepper and celery. Fill the peppers with this mixture and place them in a baking pan with 1/2 inch hot water. Top with 1/4 cup bread brumbs mixed with the other 2 tablespoons of melted butter.

Bake in a moderate oven (350 degrees) until the bread crumbs on top are nicely browned—about 30 minutes. This recipe serves 4 people.

Special Cooking School Cabbage Rolls

1 head cabbage, medium
Boiling water to cover cabbage
1 pound beef, ground
1/2 cup rice, uncooked
1 small onion, chopped
1 egg
1/2 cup cheese, grated
1 tablespoon salt
3-1/2 cups tomatoes, cooked
Cinnamon, as needed

Cut the hard center core from the cabbage. Put the head of cabbage in a pot of boiling water and cook for 5 minutes. Take cabbage out of the pot and allow to cool. Then carefully separate the leaves. Now mix the ground beef, rice, onion, egg, cheese and salt in a wooden mixing bowl. Place one heaping tablespoon of this meat mixture on each cabbage leaf. Fold one side of each cabbage leaf over towards the center and roll tightly up. Place these filled cabbage meat rolls in a lightly greased baking pan. Pour the tomatoes over this and sprinkle lightly with cinnamon. Bake in a moderate oven (350 degrees) for 1 hour. Serves 8 people.

Sweet Potato Pork Pie

1-1/2 pounds pork
1 bay leaf
6 peppercorns
2 teaspoons salt
1 stalk celery, cut into chunks

3 sprigs parsley
2 onions, chopped
2 tablespoons shortening
2 tablespoons flour
1 cup pork stock

Cut the pork into small pieces and put into a cast iron skillet. Pour on enough water to cover the meat. Then add the bay leaf, peppercorns, salt, celery and parsley. Cook until tender. Strain off the liquid and set it aside. Now sauté the onions in the shortening until they turn yellow. Add a little flour and stir until smooth. Add the pork stock gradually and cook until smooth and thickened, stirring constantly. Blend all of these ingredients together. Arrange alternate layers of this mixture and apples in a casserole greased with shortening. Set this aside and make the sweet potato crust as follows:

1 cup flour, sifted
3 teaspoons baking powder
1-1/2 teaspoons salt
3 tablespoons shortening
1 cup sweet potatoes, mashed
1/4 cup milk

Sift the flour, baking powder and salt together. Cut in the shortening with a fork. Add the sweet potatoes and milk to make a soft dough. Knead lightly on a floured surface for 20 seconds and then roll it out to a 1/2 inch thickness. Cut with a biscuit cutter and neatly arrange the pieces on top of the pie. Bake in a very hot oven (450 degrees) for 30 minutes. This grand old recipe serves 6 people.

Brunswick Stew

1 chicken, cut up
3 teaspoons salt
1/4 cup butter
2 onions, sliced

2-1/2 cups tomatoes, stewed
3/4 cup tomato paste
2 cups bouillon or
2 cups consommé
1 cup celery with leaves, finely diced
1/4 teaspoon marjoram
1/4 teaspoon thyme
1/2 cup corn, cooked
1-1/4 cups lima beans, cooked
3 tablespoons butter
2 tablespoons flour

Sprinkle the chicken pieces with 1 teaspoon of the salt. Melt the butter in a deep cast iron kettle. Brown the pieces of chicken and then remove them from the pot. Add the onions and brown lightly. Return the chicken pieces to the kettle. Add in the tomatoes, tomato paste, bouillon or consommé, celery, marjoram, thyme and the remaining salt. Stir well, cover and let simmer for 1 hour. Now add the corn and lima beans and let simmer for 20 minutes longer. Melt the butter and blend in with the flour. Add a cup of the liquid from the stew and stir this until smooth. Blend this with the stew and cook for 2 minutes. This recipe will feed 6 people.

Mary Lincoln's Prize Cooked Salad Dressing

1 egg
2 tablespoons sugar
1 teaspoon salt
1 teaspoon mustard

2 tablespoons flour
3/4 cup milk
1/4 cup vinegar
1 tablespoon butter

Beat the egg slightly in a saucepan. Then add the sugar, salt, mustard, flour and milk. Stir until smooth. Slowly blend in the vinegar. Stir while cooking over a very low heat, for 10 minutes, until thickened. Remove from the stove and stir in the butter. Cool quickly and keep refrigerated until ready to use. This recipe makes 1-1/4 cups.

Famous Boston Baked Beans

2 cups navy beans, dry
6 cups water
1/4 pound salt pork, sliced
1-1/2 teaspoons salt
1/4 cup brown sugar, packed
1 teaspoon dry mustard
2 teaspoons onion, chopped
1/2 cup dark molasses

Put the beans into a pot, add the water and let boil for 2 minutes. Then take them off the stove and let them soak for 1 hour. Now add the salt pork and salt to the beans and simmer until the beans are tender. This will take about 1-1/2 hours. Drain and save 1 cup of the liquid. Put the beans into a baking pan. Meanwhile, combine the liquid saved from the beans and the brown sugar, mustard, onion and molasses. Pour this mixture over the beans and bake uncovered in a moderate oven (350 degrees) for 1 hour, or until the beans are lightly browned on top and of the desired consistency.

For a great variation of the above dish, you may add the following ingredients:

1/2 cup ham pieces
2 tablespoons bacon grease
1/2 cup catsup
1/2 bell pepper, chopped
1/8 teaspoon nutmeg

Instead of baking, you may simply simmer these beans for 35 minutes on top of the stove, or until the beans are of the desired consistency. Stir only as necessary to avoid sticking.

Baked Stuffed Fish

1 dressed fish, 3 pounds
1 teaspoon pepper
2 teaspoons salt
2 tablespoons butter, melted

Wash and dry the fish. Then sprinkle the inside with the salt and pepper. Use more if desired. Place the fish on a well-greased baking pan. Now proceed to make the stuffing:

3 tablespoons butter
3/4 cup celery, chopped
2 tablespoons onion, chopped
4 cups soft breadcrumbs
1/2 teaspoon salt
1/4 teaspoon pepper
1/2 cup nuts, chopped

Melt the butter in a cast iron skillet. Put in the celery and onion and cook for 3 minutes. Take off the stove and add all the other ingredients and mix well. Stuff the fish loosely and then brush the outside with melted butter. Any extra dressing may be baked in the same pan with the fish. Bake in a moderate oven (350 degrees) for from 45 to 60 minutes, or until the fish flakes easily when tested with a fork.

Unbeatable Homemade Coffee Can Nut Bread

4 cups flour
1 package dry yeast

1/2 cup water
1/2 cup milk
1/2 cup butter
1/4 cup sugar
1 teaspoon salt
1/2 cup almonds, ground
1/2 cup raisins, chopped
2 eggs, slightly beaten

Blend 2 cups of the flour with the yeast in a large wooden mixing bowl. Take a saucepan and combine the water, milk, butter, sugar and salt. Cook over a low heat until the butter is completely melted. Let this cool for 5 minutes and then stir it into the flour-yeast mixture in the bowl. Now add the balance of the flour, the nuts, raisins and eggs. Blend well. The dough will be stiff. Knead on a floured surface until the dough is smooth and elastic. Divide the dough in half and put it in two greased 1-pound coffee cans. Cover the cans loosely with the plastic tops. Let the dough rise in a warm place (85 degrees) until the dough reaches to 1 inch from the top of the cans. Remove the plastic tops and bake in a moderate oven (375 degrees) for 35 minutes, or until browned and the bread sounds hollow when tapped with the finger. This recipe makes two 1-pound loaves of delightful coffee-can bread.

Interior of a Colonial kitchen, in home of Royal Governor William Tryon, New Bern, North Carolina. This home was visited by George Washington, and is called Tryon Palace. *Courtesy of State Department of Archives and History, Raleigh, North Carolina.*

Bibliography of Interesting Old Cook Books

American Orphan.[1] *American Cookery.* Brattleboro, Vt.: 1819.

An American Lady. *New American Cookery or Female Companion.* New York: 1805.

Andrew's Pearl Offering Devoted to Etiquette and Decorum, Toilet and Cooking Recipes and Information for Everybody. Chicago: C.E. Andrews & Company, 1881.

Anonymous. *The Compleat Cook.* London: 1664.

Blakeslee, Mrs. E.C. *Compendium of Cookery and Reliable Recipes.* Chicago: Merchant's Specialty Company, 1890.

Boston Housekeeper, A. *The Cooks Own Book: Being a Complete Culinary Encyclopedia.* Boston: Munroe and Francis, 1832.

Bradley, Martha. *The British Housewife: or, the Cook, Housekeeper's and Gardner's Companion.*[2] London: 1770.

Bradley, Richard. *Bradley's Country Housewife.* London: 1772.

_____. *The Country Housewife and Lady's Director.* London: 1727.

Bride's Book of Recipes and Household Hints, The. St. Paul, Minnesota: Carlton J. West, 1875.

Briggs, Richard. *English Art of Cookery.* London: 1794.

Brown, Charles W. *Standard Cyclopedia of Recipes.* Chicago: Frederick Drake & Company, 1901.

Burt, Elizabeth. *Cook Book.*[3] Handwritten manuscript, unpublished. Fort Laramie, Wyoming: 1870.

Carter, Susannah. *The Frugal Housewife.*[4] Boston: 1772.

Chase, A.W. *Dr. Chase's Recipes: Or Information for Everybody.* Ann Arbor, Michigan: R.A. Beal, 1870.

Child, Mrs. *The American Frugal Housewife.* Boston: 1835.

Cocoa and Chocolate. Dorchester, Massachusetts: Walter Baker & Company, 1886.

Colliers Cyclopedia of Commercial and Social Information. "Hints to Housekeepers," pp. 662-674. New York: P.F. Collier, Publisher, 1882.

Complete Bread, Cake and Cracker Baker, The. Chicago: Confectioner and Baker Publishing Company, 1881.

Confederate Receipt Book. Richmond: West and Johnson, 1863.

Cornelius, Mrs. *The Young Housekeeper's Friend.* Boston: 1840.

Courtney, Sarah Delphine Halsey. *Cook Book Receipts.* New York: Handwritten manuscript, 1873.

Crowen, Mrs. T.J. *American Lady's Cookery Book.* New York: 1866.

Custis, Frances Parke.[5] *A Booke of Cookery.*[6] Handwritten, leather-bound manuscript containing numbered entries 1 through 206.

_____. *A Booke of Sweetmeats.* Handwritten, leather-bound manuscript containing numbered entries 1 through 326.

Davis, E.B. and Professor B.G. Jefferies, M.D., Ph.D. *The Household Guide: or Home Remedies and Home Treatment.* Naperville, Illinois: J.L. Nichols Publisher, 1891.

Everybody's Cook and Receipt Book: But More Particularly Designed for Buckeyes, Hoosiers, Wolverines, Corncrackers, Suckers, And All Epicures Who Wish To Live With The Present Times. Cleveland, Ohio: 1842.

Family Receipt Book and Medical Advice. New York: A.L. Scovill Company, 1852.

Glasse, Hannah. *The Complete Confectioner.* London: Published sometime during the mid-1700s.

Hall, T. *Queens Royal Cookery.* London: 1719.

Harland, Marion. *Breakfast, Luncheon and Tea.* New York: Scribner, Armstrong & Company, 1875.

_____. *Common Sense in the Household—A Manual of Practical Housewifery.* New York: 1871.

Harrison, Sarah. *The House-Keeper's Pocket-Book, and Compleat Family Cook.*[7] London: 1733.

Henderson, Mary F. *Practical Cooking and Dinner Giving.* New York: 1876.

Henderson, W.A. *Modern Domestic Cookery.* Boston: 1847.

Housekeeper, A. *Practical American Cook Book.* New York: 1855.

Housekeeper's Companion: A Practical Recipe Book, The. Chicago: Mercantile Publishing and Advertising Company, 1883.

Howland, E.A. *The Practical Cook Book.* Boston: 1865.

Inquire Within for Anything You Want to Know. New York: Garrett, Dick & Fitzgerald, 1858.

Kansas Home Cook Book, The. Leavenworth, Kansas: Board of Managers, 1874.

Lady, A. *The Art of Cookery Made Plain and Easy.*[8] London: 1747.

Leslie, Miss. *Seventy-Five Receipts.* Boston: 1827.

_____. *The Cook's Own Book.* New York: 1865.

Lyman, Joseph B. and Laura E. Lyman. *The Philosophy of Housekeeping.* New York: 1867.

Markham, Gervase. *Countrey Contentments: Or The English Housewife.* London: 1623.

May, Robert. *The Accomplish't Cook, Or the Art & Mystery of Cookery.* London: 1660.

Montana Cook Book. Butte City, Montana: Edited by the ladies of Butte City, 1881.

Morris, Elizabeth. *Cook Book.* Ithaca, New York: Handwritten manuscript, 1850.

Parloa, Maria. *The Applecore Cook Book.* Boston: Estes and Lauriat Company, 1872.

Practical Housekeeping. Minneapolis: Buckeye Publishing, 1884.

Presbyterian Cook Book, The. Dayton, Ohio: Historical Publishing Company, 1886.

Putnam, Mrs. E. *Mrs. Putnam's Receipt Book.* New York: Sheldon & Company, 1867.

Raffald, Mrs. *The Experienced English House-Keeper, for the Use and Ease of Ladies, House-keepers, Cooks, etc.*[9] Manchester, England, 1769.

Randolph, Mrs. Mary.[10] *The Virginia Housewife: or, Methodical Cook.* Richmond, Virginia: 1824.[11]

Rorer, Sarah Tyson.[12] *Home Candy Making.* Philadelphia: Arnold & Company, 1889.

_____. *Mrs. Rorer's New Cook Book: A Manual of Housekeeping.* Philadelphia: Arnold & Company, 1898.

_____. *Mrs. Rorer's Philadelphia Cook Book.* Philadelphia: Arnold & Company, 1886.

Royal Baker and Pastry Book, The. New York: The Royal Baking Powder Company, 1890.

Scovil, Elisabeth Robinson. *A Baby's Requirements.* Philadelphia: Henry Altemus, 1892.

Simmons, Amelia. *American Cookery.*[13] Hartford, Connecticut: Hudson and Goodwin, 1796.

Smiley's Cook Book and Universal Household Guide. Chicago: Smiley Publishing Company, 1894.

Smith, E. *The Compleat Housewife: or, Accomplish'd Gentlewoman's Companion.*[14] Williamsburg, Virginia: William Parks, 1742.

Smith, Mary Stuart. *Virginia Cookery-Book.* New York: Harper's Franklin Square Library, 1881.

Texas Cook Book. Houston: First Presbyterian Church, 1880.

Thurber, Francis B. *Coffee from Plantation to Cup.* New York: American Grocers Publishing Association, 1881.

Trall, Dr. R.T. *The New Hydrophathic Cook Book.* New York: Samuel R. Wells, 1873.

Tyree, Marion Cabell. *Housekeeping in Old Virginia.* Louisville, Kentucky: 1879.

Washington, Martha. *Rules for Cooking.* Handwritten manuscript containing over 500 recipe entries collected by Martha.

Widdifield, Hannah. *Practical Receipts for the Housewife.* Philadelphia: 1856.

Winslow, Mrs. *Mrs. Winslow's Domestic Receipt Book.* Boston: George C. Rand & Avery, 1862.

Wright, Julia McNair. *The Complete Home: An Encyclopedia of Domestic Life and Affairs.* Philadelphia: J.C. McCurdy & Company, Ltd., 1879.

Zieber, G.B. *Chamber's Information for the People.* Philadelphia: J. & J.L. Giron, 1846.

FOOTNOTES

1. A later version of Amelia Simmons' cook book, which was originally published in 1796.

2. A very popular cook book in early Virginia.

3. Mrs. Burt's *Cook Book* is in the possession of the National Park Service, Fort Laramie Historical Site, Fort Laramie, Wyoming.

4. Paul Revere made the plates for this British cook book when it was first published in America.

5. Mother of Martha Washington's first husband. She was formerly Mrs. Daniel Custis. She gave her recipes to Martha, who later handed them down to Nellie Custis, her granddaughter.

6. Presently in the archives of Pennsylvania Historical Society.

7. A very popular early Virginia cook book. A copy can be found in the Research Library at Williamsburg, Virginia. Sold in 1760s and 1770s at the Virginia Gazette's office in Williamsburg.

8. This was the best selling 18th century cook book in the Colonies. First American edition published in Alexandria, Virginia, in 1805. The 4th edition revealed it was written by Hannah Glasse, believed to be a pseudonym of Dr. John Hull, a London writer.

9. One of the most popular cook books in early Virginia.

10. Mary Randolph was reputed to be the best cook in Richmond. Her cook book was the first ever published in the South. William and Mary College owns a first edition copy.

11. Later published in Philadelphia, E.H. Butler & Co., 1860.

12. Mrs. Rorer was the Culinary Editor for the Ladie's Home Journal from 1897 to 1908.

13. First originally American cook book ever published in America. It was a 48 page paperback.

14. One of the first cook books printed in British controlled America. Reprinted again in New York, 1764.

Old-Time Measurements

1 wineglass = 4 tablespoons; 1/2 gill; 1/4 cup
4 wineglasses = 1 cup
1 teacup = 3/4 cup
2/3 teacup = 1/2 cup
1/3 teacup = 1/4 cup
1 kitchen cup = 1 cup; 2 gills
1 coffee cup = 1 cup; 2 gills
1 tin cup = 1 cup; 2 gills
1 tumblerfull = 2 cups
1 gram = 1/5 teaspoon
1 dram liquid = 3/4 teaspoon
1 dessert spoon = 2 teaspoons
2 dessert spoons = 1 tablespoon
1 salt spoon = 1/4 teaspoon
4 salt spoons = 1 teaspoon
Pinch of salt = 1/8 teaspoon
Dash of pepper = 3 good shakes; 1/8 teaspoon
Lump of butter = 1 well rounded tablespoon
Butter the size of an egg = 2 tablespoons; 1/4 cup
Butter the size of a walnut = 1 tablespoon

Pound of butter = 2 cups
Pound of eggs = 2 cups; 8 large eggs (without shells); 10 medium eggs (without shells); 12 small eggs (without shells).
Quart of eggs = 4 cups; 16 large eggs (without shells); 20 medium eggs (without shells); 24 small eggs (without shells).
Pint of eggs = 2 cups; 8 large eggs (without shells); 10 medium eggs (without shells); 12 small eggs (without shells).
1/2 pint eggs = 1 cup; 4 large eggs (without shells); 5 medium eggs (without shells); 6 small eggs (without shells).
Pound of sugar = 2 cups
Pound of milk = 2 cups
Pound of corn meal (coarse) = 3 cups
Pound of corn meal (fine) = 4 cups
Pound of ground suet = 4 cups
Pound of flour = 4 cups
Pound of powdered sugar = 2-1/2 cups

Pound of candied fruit = 1-1/2 cups
Pound of rye flour = 5 cups
Pound of whole wheat flour = 3-1/2 cups
Pound of oatmeal = 4 cups
Pound of dry beans = 2 cups
A heaping quart sifted flour = 1 pound
1/4 gill = 2 tablespoons
1/2 gill = 4 tablespoons; 1/4 cup
1 gill = 1/2 cup
2 gills = 1 cup
1/4 peck = 2 quarts; 8 cups
1 peck = 8 quarts
2/3 cups liquid yeast = 1/2 cake compressed
   yeast
1 grated lemon rind = 1 tablespoon
1 grated orange rind = 3 tablespoons
1 drachm = 1/2 tablespoon liquid; 1/4 tablespoon
   dry ingredients.
1/2 pint = 1 cup
1 pint = 2 cups
1 quart = 4 cups
3 teaspoons = 1 tablespoon
4 tablespoons = 1/4 cup

INDEX

Adams, Abigail, 131
Adams, John, 129, 131
Adams, John Quincy, 137
Ale Fritters, 55
Allen, Ethan, 31
Almond and Raisin Bread, 126, 127
Almond White Cake, 129, 130
Apache Stew, 89
Apple Baked Dish, 92
Apple Catsup, 45
Apple Coffeecake, 27
Apple Dressing, 125
Apple Fritters, 67
Apple Pastries To Fry, 4
Apple Pudding, 22

Baked Ham and Apples, 33
Baked Stuffed Fish, 156, 157
Bancroft, George, 147
Barlowe, Arthur, 3
Bean Balls, 92
Beauregard, General Pierre, 104
Beef Soup, 76
Beef Steak, 21
Beef Steak and Oysters, 75
Black Drink, 93

Blaine, James Gillespie, 143
Boiled Custard of 1810, 132
Boiled Icing, 129, 130
Bonney, William Henry, 75
Boone, Daniel, 97
Boston Baked Beans, 69, 156
Boston Cooking School, 10, 149-157
Boston Cream Pie, 60
Bread and Butter Molasses Pudding, 83, 84
Bread Pudding, 37, 38
Brown Beans and Dumplings, 82
Brown Bread, 120
Brown, John, 98
Brown Sugar Fudge, 145
Brunswick Stew, 154, 155
Buchanan, James, 129
Burt, Elizabeth, 71, 72, 159

Cabbage Dish, 80
Cabbage Rolls, 153
Cabbage Soup, 143
Candied Sweet Potatoes, 142
Carr, Camillus, 82
Carson, Kit, 81
Cauliflower Dish, 26
Cheese Pudding, 19

Chicken and Tomato Delight, 115
Chicken Croquettes, 117, 118
Chicken Kiev, 39
Chicken Pudding, 42
Chicken Salad, 71, 72
Chicken Scrapple, 79
Chocolate Sauce, 38
Chops and Potato Casserole, 39
Clam Bake, 88
Clam Chowder, 59
Clam Soup, 140
Codfish Balls, 64
Cody, William Frederick (Buffalo Bill), 80
Coffee Can Nut Bread, 157
Coffee Ice Cream, 14
Coffee Soufflé, 146
Colonial Onion Soup, 11, 12
Colonial Potato Omelet, 15
Cooked Salad Dressing, 155
Corn Bread, 43, 77, 120
Corn Fondue Pudding, 150
Corn Muffins, 98
Corn Pancakes, 149
Corn Pudding, 31
Corn Relish, 35

Corned Beef and Cabbage, 61
Corson, Juliet, 10, 141-148
Creamy Rice Pudding, 100
Creole Corn Muffins, 98
Crockett, Davy, 23
Crullers, 101
Cucumber Soup, 54
Currant Loaf, 68
Cushing, William Barker, 123
Custer, General George Armstrong, 74, 87
Custis, Francis Parke, 47, 160
Custis, Nellie (Eleanor Parke), 47, 50
Cutlets a la Jefferson, 44

Dakota Fried Tomatoes, 74
Davis, Jefferson, 99, 100
Davis, Varna, 99
Delicate Fritters, 134
Doughnuts—A Yankee Cake, 8
Douglass, Frederick, 111
Dutch Pepper Salad, 119

Egg and Tomato Bake, 40
Eggplant Salad, 126
Eggplant, Stuffed, 99
Elkswatawa, 86
Ellery, William, 23
Endicott, John, 19
Evart, William, 60
Excellent Pancakes, 48

Farmer, Fanny, 149
Fat Rascals, 144
Fish, Stuffed, 156, 157
Fish Timbales, 102
Flannel Cakes, 110
Foamy Sauce, 50
Fort Laramie Chicken Salad, 71, 72
Fox, George, 17
Fremont, John, 81, 143
French Chicken Kiev, 39
French Custard, 41
French Veronique, 103
Fresh Corn Bread, 120
Fried Squash Blossoms, 93
Fried Tomatoes, 74, 128
Frosted Tea Cookies, 137
Frying Pan Boiled Liver, 150

Garrison, William Lloyd, 68, 69
Gates, General Horatio, 34
Gatling, Richard Jordan, 106
Geronimo, 89
Ginger Bread, 65
Ginger Cookies, 63
Goose, Roast, 125
Grant, Frederick Dent, 119
Grant, Julia Dent, 135
Grant, Ulysses S., 75, 119, 135
Grape Salad, 139
Green Corn Pudding, 31

Greene, Nathanael, 61
Gresham, Walter Quinton, 121

Ham and Cider, 109
Ham and Egg Pie, 18
Ham and Parsnips, 51
Ham Croquettes, 112
Hampton, Wade, 105
Harrison, William Henry, 138
Hasty Pudding, 5
Hendrick, Chief, 90
Herb Omelette, 30
Homemade Bread, 94
Hood, John Bell, 95, 96
Horseradish Vinegar, 40
Hot Egg Salad, 141, 142
Houston, Sam, 73

Imperial Macaroni Delight, 148
Indian Apple Baked Dish, 92
Indian Clam Bake, 88
Indian Pudding, 5, 81

Jackson, Andrew, 129, 139
Jackson, Rachel, 139
Jefferson, Martha, 40, 42, 44, 47
Jefferson, Thomas, 37-46
Johnny Cake Meal Pudding, 57, 58
Jones, John Paul, 26
Joseph, Chief, 94

Kansas Chicken Scrapple, 79
Kearney, General, 79
King, Rufus, 67
Kinnison, David, 62
Kirkland, Samuel, 68
Koo Wes Koo We, 83, 84

LaFayette, General, 30
Lamb and Lentil Pottage, 152
Lamb Casserole, 54
Leather Britches, 87
Lee, Richard Henry, 32, 33
Lee, Robert E., 102
Lincoln, Abraham, 129, 130
Lincoln, Mary, 10, 149-157
Liver, Boiled, 150
Liver Dish, 145
Lobster Salad, 131
Logan, John Alexander, 128
Loudoun, John Campbell, 22
Lyon, Nathaniel, 65

Madison, Dolly, 132
Madison, James, 132
Mashed Parsnips, 13
Meat Fold-Overs, 122
Mexican Corn Bread Deluxe, 77
Midwestern Steamed Brown Bread, 120
Mince Meat, 52
Molasses Cake, 16

Molasses Candy, 111
Monroe, Elizabeth, 134
Monroe, James, 134
Montana Blind Rabbit, 75
Morris, Robert, 29
Motte, Rebecca, 13
Mousse of Crab Meat, 144
Muhlenberg, John, 27
Mushroom-Chicken Loaf, 135

Navaho Bean Balls, 92
New England Boiled Dinner, 66
New England Clam Chowder, 59

Oglethorpe, James, 16
Oklahoma Territory Beef Soup, 76
Onion Soup, 11, 12
Osceola, Chief, 93
Owens, Francis E., 141, 148
Oyster Dish, 138
Oyster Fricassee, 147
Oyster Ketchup, 62
Oyster Sauce for Roast Chicken, 49

Pack Mule Indian Pudding, 81
Paine, Thomas, 23
Peale, Charles Wilson, 53
Penn, William, 15
Pepper Hash, 146, 147
Pepper Salad, 119

Pickering, Timothy, 28
Pierce, Franklin, 140
Plantation Biscuits, 105
Plantation Spider Cake, 107, 108
Plantation Stew with Dumplings, 113
Plum-Peach Jam, 90
Plum Pudding, 50
Pocahontas, 91
Polk, James, 136
Pork Fruit Cake, 114
Pork Tenderloin Bouquet, 151
Potato Omelet, 15
Potato Pot Soup, 20
Potato Puffs, 110
Pound Cake, 104
Powell, Willis, 93
Pumpkin Custard, 28
Pumpkin Pie, 51
Pumpkin Soup, 85
Putnam, Israel, 33

Quaker Pudding, 17

Randolph, John, 91
Randolph, Mary, 8, 161
Randolph, William, 91
Raspberry Royal, 136
Red Bean Soup, 133
Red Jacket, 85
Reed, Joseph, 14

Rhode Island Johnny Cake
    Meal Pudding, 57, 58
Rice Popovers, 34
Rice Pudding, 100
Roast Goose with Apple Dressing, 125
Robertson, James, 101
Rochambeau, Count Jean, 23, 24
Ross, John, 84
Ruffin, Edmund, 103

Sagoyewatha, 85
Salad Dressing, 106, 155
Salmon and Tomato, 124
Salt Cured Ham and Cider, 109
Savory Cheese Pudding, 19
Scalloped Oysters, 95, 96
Schuyler, John P., 35
Scott, General Winfield, 77
Scripture Cake, 116
Shepherd's Pie, 124
Shrimp Fantasy, 123
Simmons, Amelia, 5, 6, 161
Sitting Bull, 87
Skillet Cookies, 78
Smith, E., 4, 162
Sour Cream Dressing, 144
Southern Fried Chicken, 97
Spicy Chicken, 127
Spinach Ring, 121
Squash Blossoms, 93

Squash Doughnuts, 45
Squaw Cake, 86
Starr, Belle, 76
Stephens, Alexander, 100
Stewed Apple Coffeecake, 27
Stewed Beets, 138
Stewed Mushrooms, 23, 24
Stuffed Eggplant, 99
Stuffed Fish, 156, 157
Stuffed Meat Loaf, 32
Stuffed Peppers, 152
Sugarless Corn Bread, 43
Sullivan, John, 20
Sumner, Charles, 64
Sweet Potato Pone, 112
Sweet Potato Pork Pie, 154

Taylor, Zachary, 129, 133
Tecumseh, 86
Texas Barbecue Sauce, 73
Todd, Mary, 130
Tomato Cocktail, 44
Trappers Fruit, 117
Trumbull, Jonathan, 21

Vallandigham, Clement L., 117, 118
Van Buren, Martin, 138
Veal Rice Pie, 56

Wade, Benjamin, 66

Walnut Gypsy Stew, 25
Washington, George, 32, 37, 48-56, 129
Washington, Martha, 47-56
Washington, Mary, 49
Wayne, General Anthony, 25
Webster, Noah, 59
Wentworth, Sir John, 11, 12
Whipple, Abraham, 57, 58
Whitney, Eli, 63
Winslow, Edward, 18
Wise, Henry Alexander, 98

Yam Loaf, 91
Yard of Flannel, 37
Yorkshire Country Captain, 53
Young, Brigham, 78

Acknowledgement

The authors are grateful to every person who helped make this book possible. Our special thanks go to Donald R. Taylor, Curator of Education, Tryon Palace, New Bern, North Carolina; Paul G. Sifton, Specialist, Early American History, Manuscript Division, the Library of Congress; and to Maurice K. Kahan, Publicity, Sleepy Hollow Restorations, Tarrytown, New York.

To these mentions we would like to add the many helpful State Historical Societies throughout the nation; the Smithsonian Institution in Washington, D.C.; Helen Duprey Bullock of the National Trust for Historic Preservation in Washington, D.C.; and the Preservation Society of New Port County, in Newport, Rhode Island.